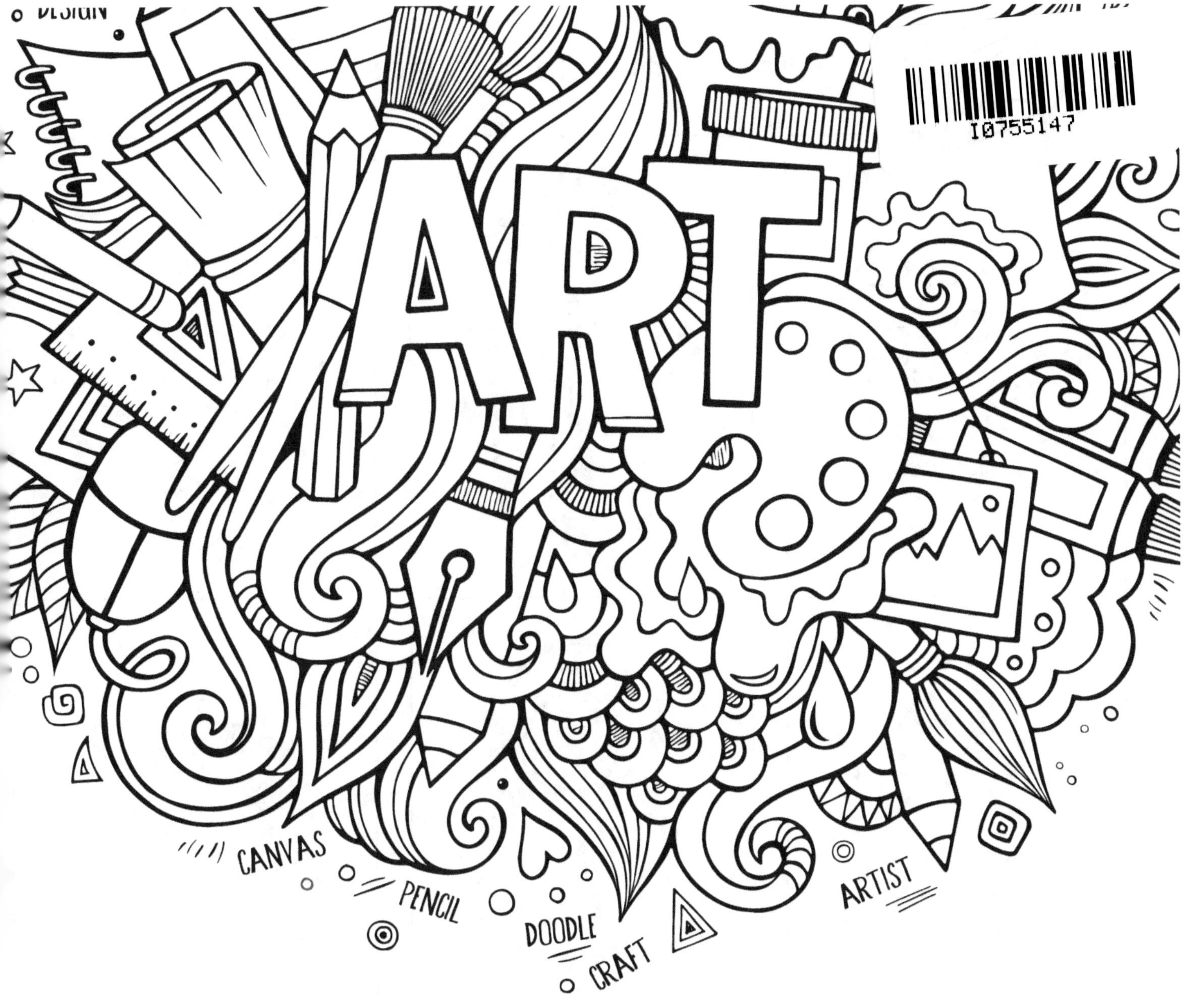

Coloring Book For Teens

Anti-Stress Designs Vol 1

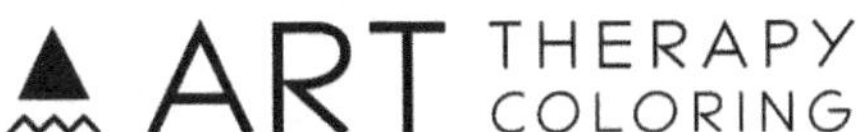

Preview of Coloring Pages

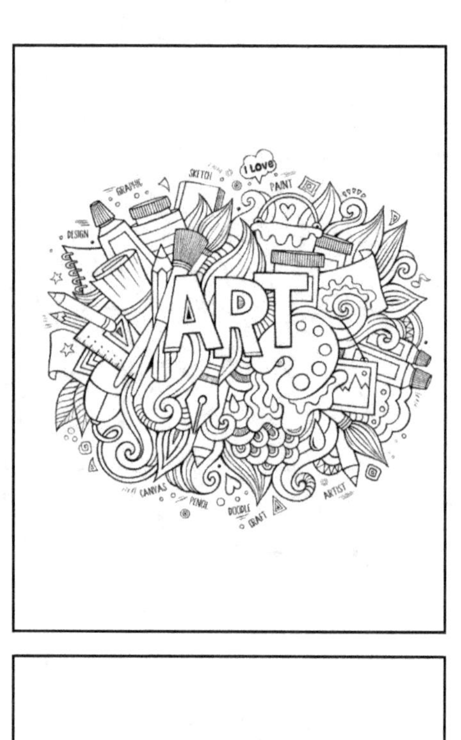

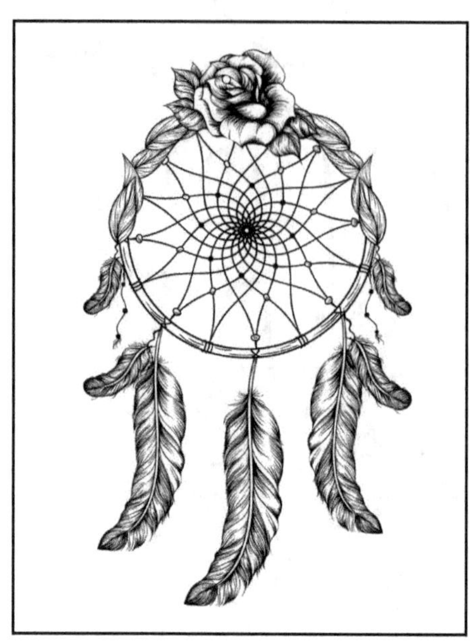

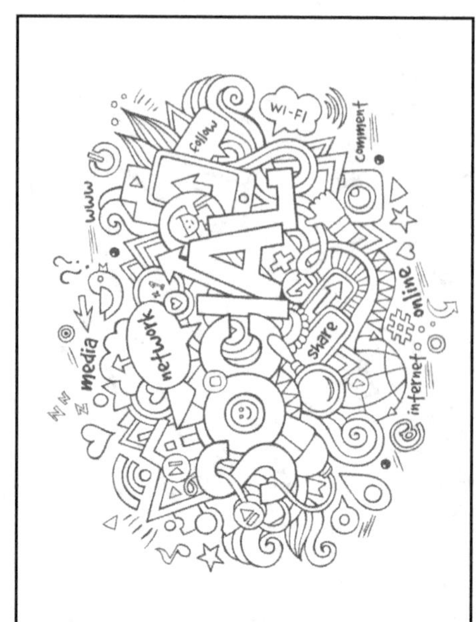

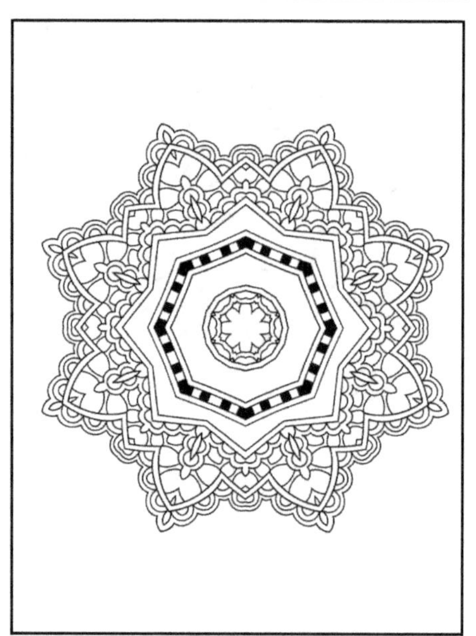

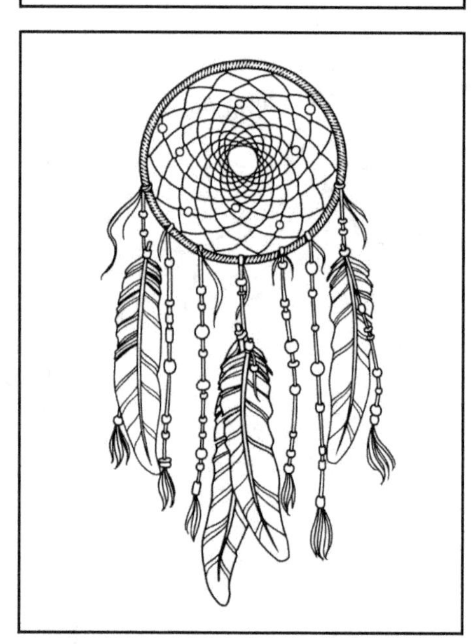

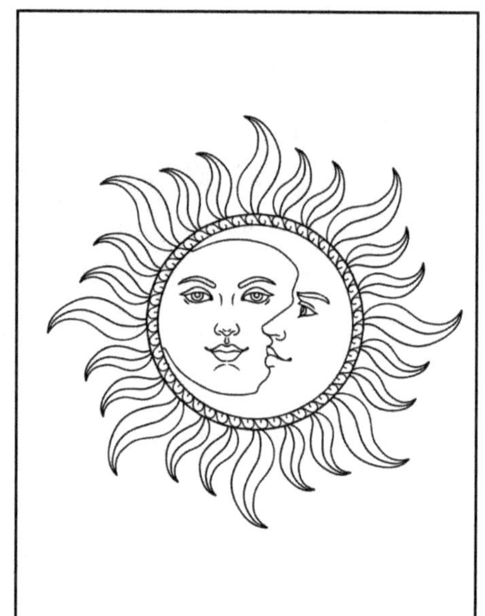

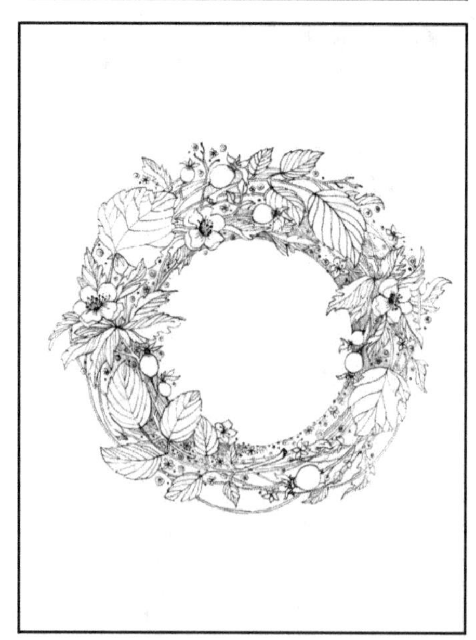

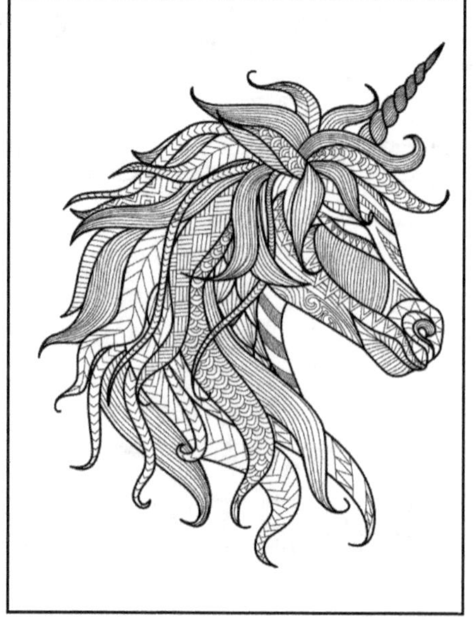

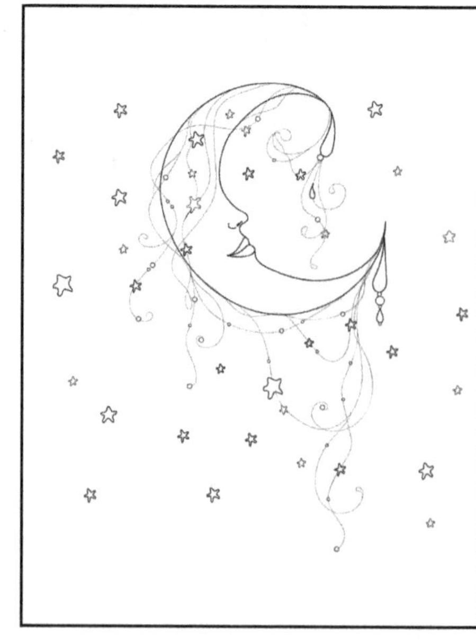

www.arttherapycoloring.com

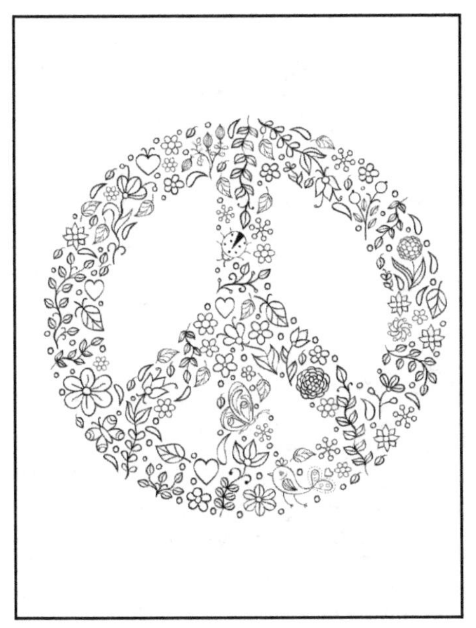
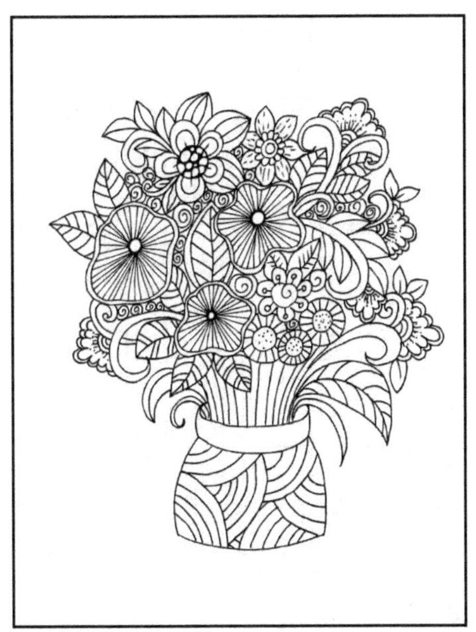
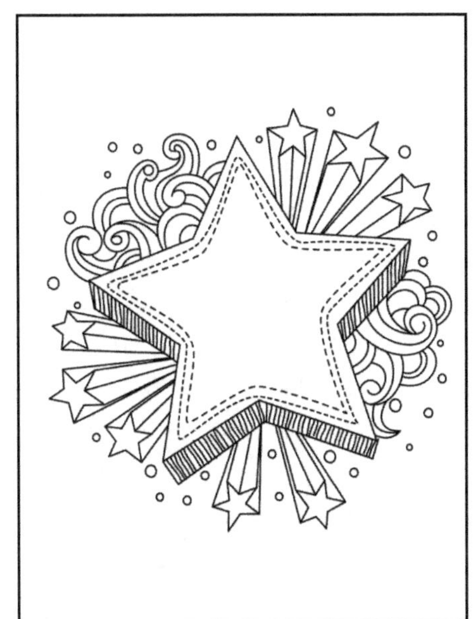
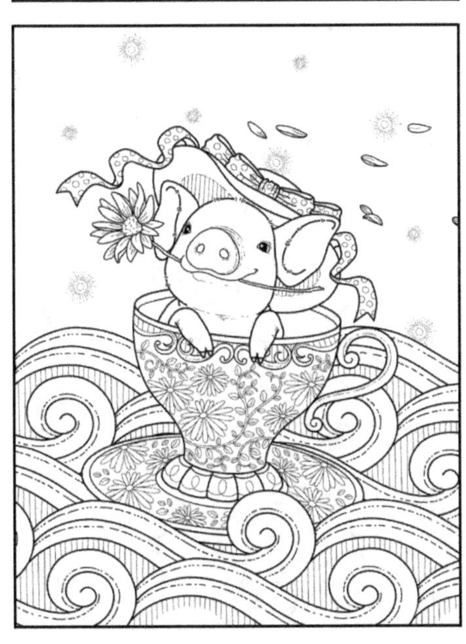
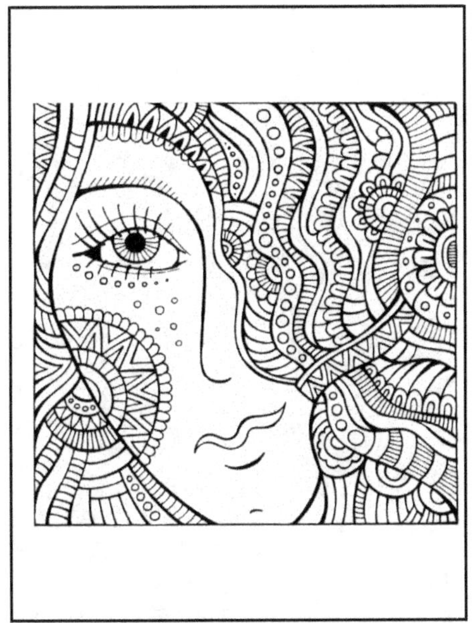
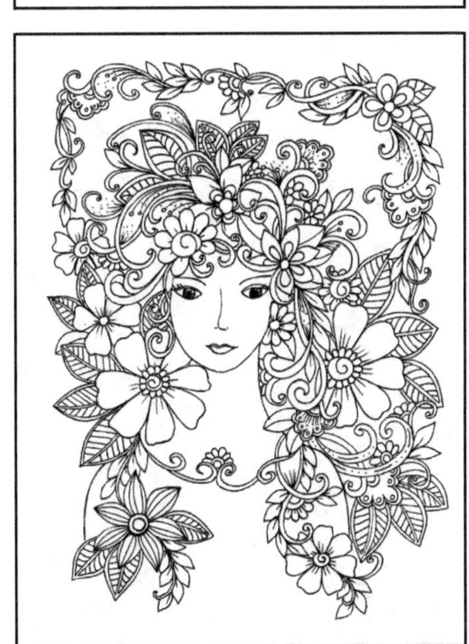
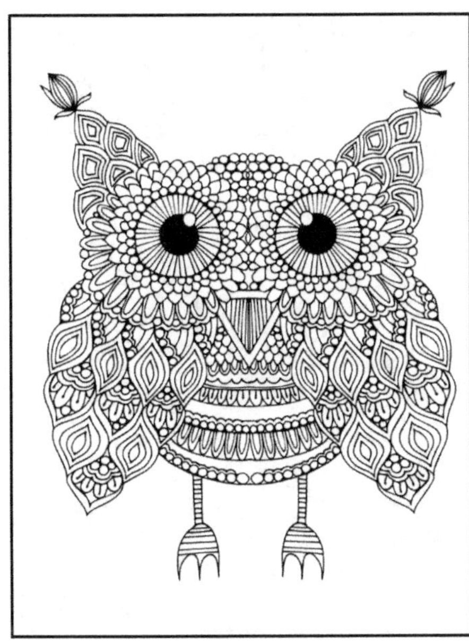
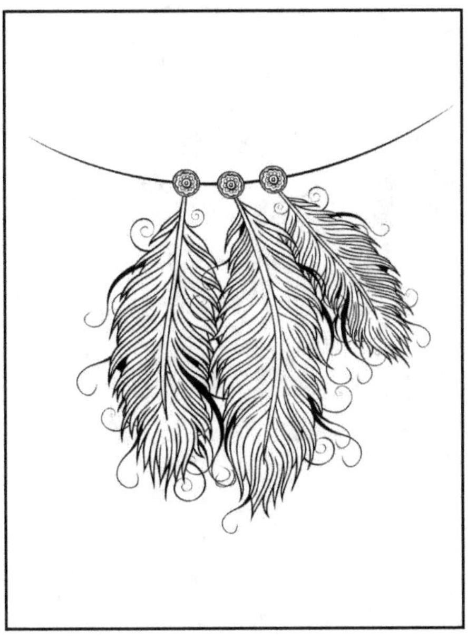
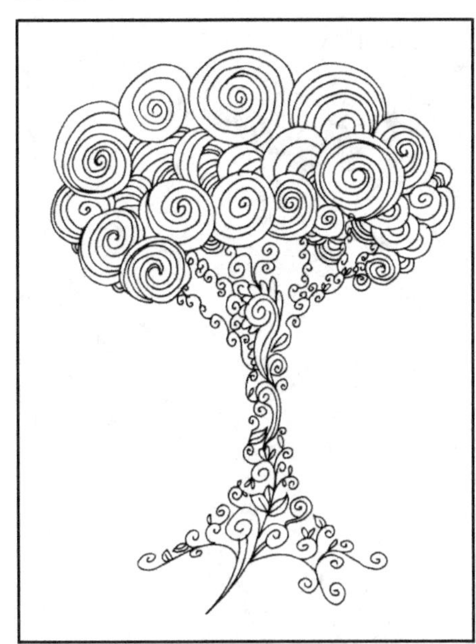

Preview of Coloring Pages

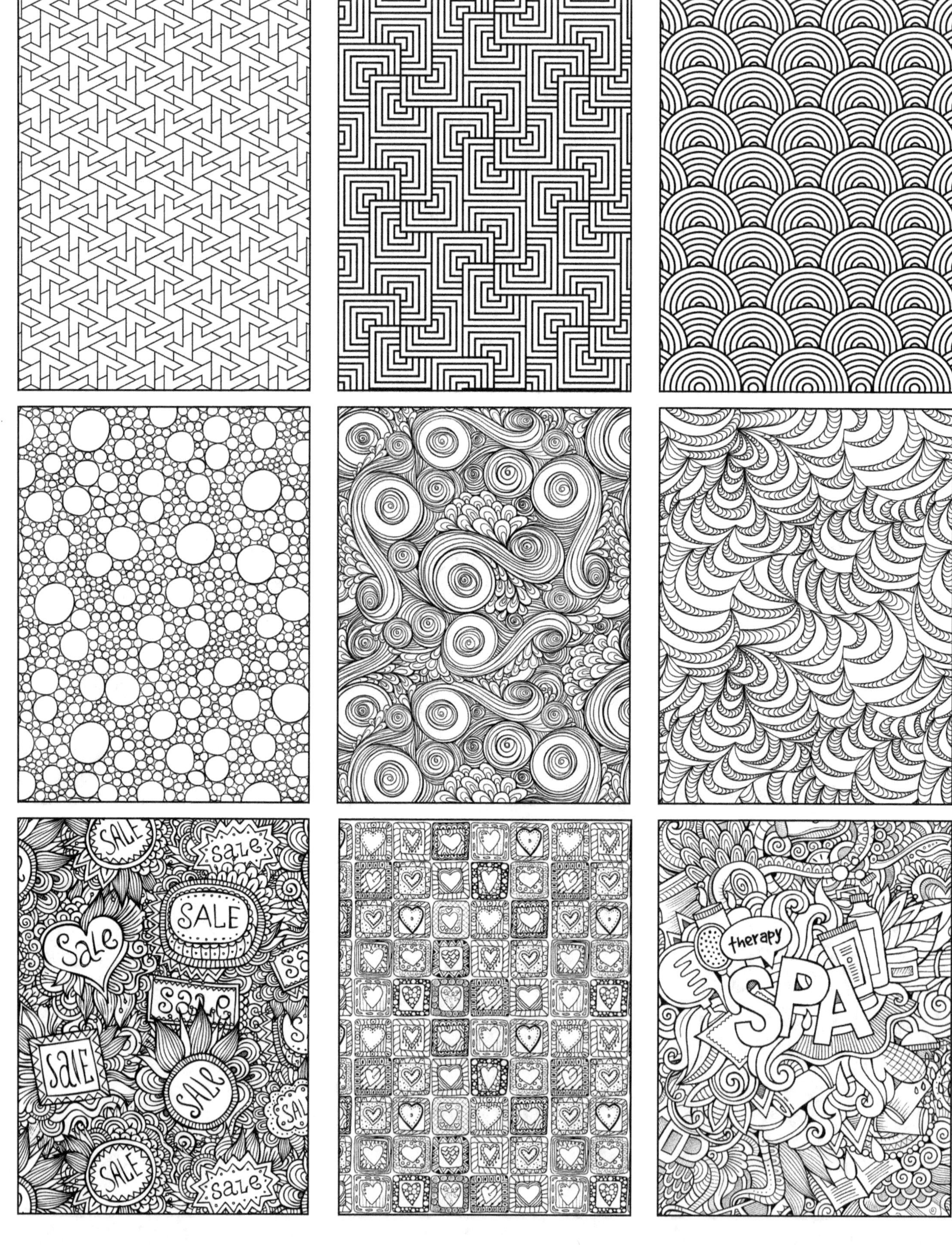

www.arttherapycoloring.com

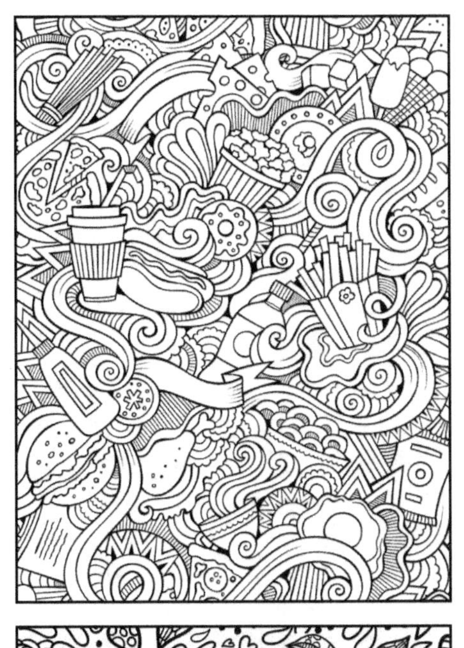

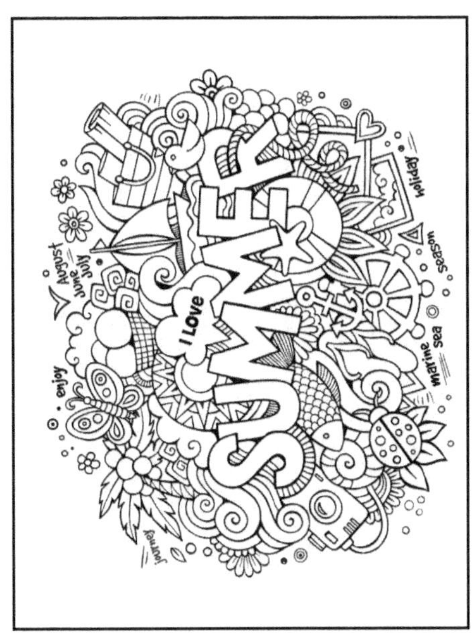

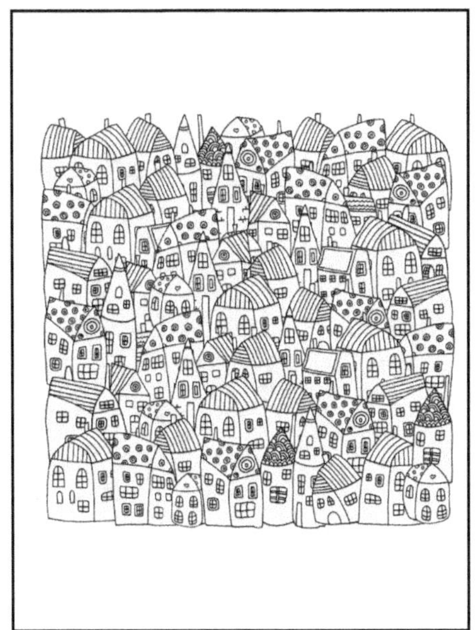

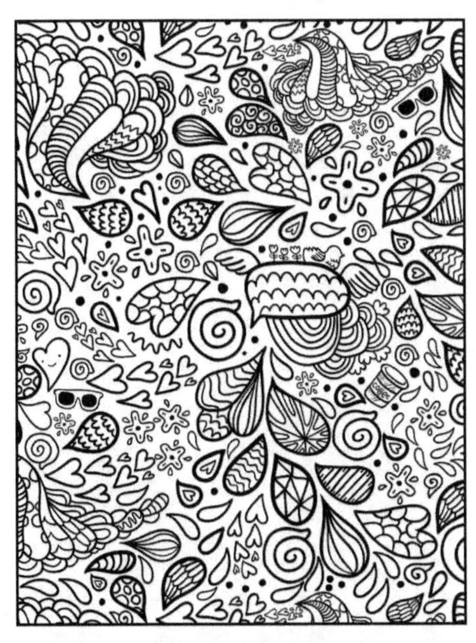

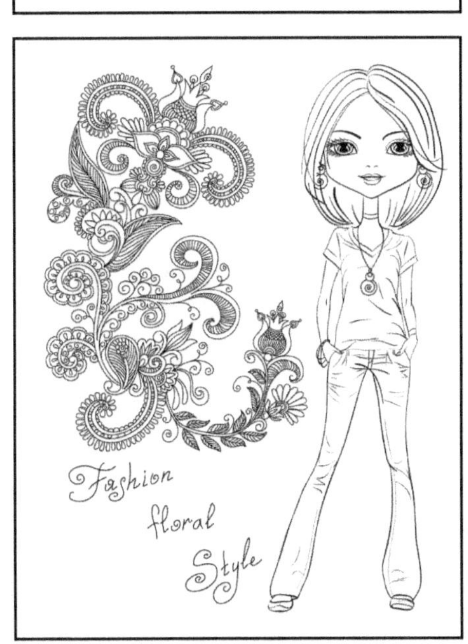

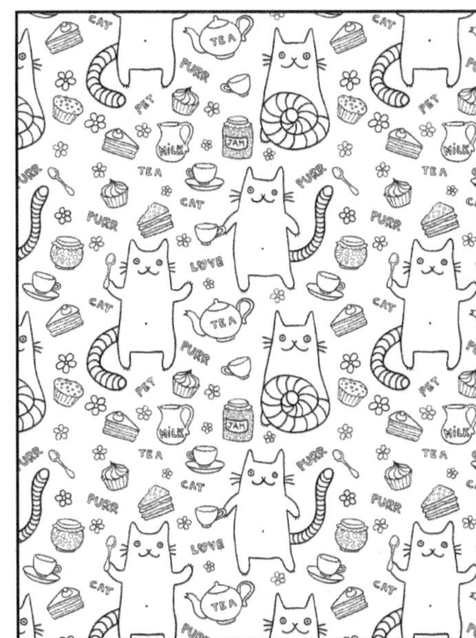

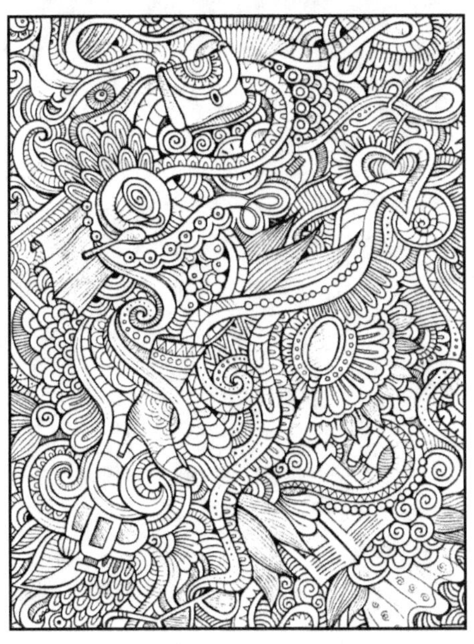

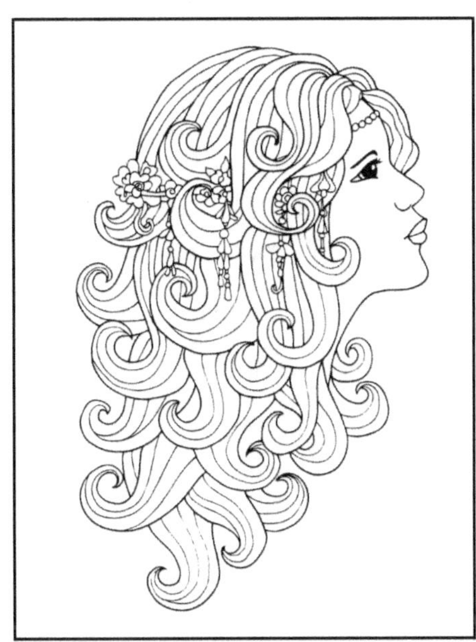

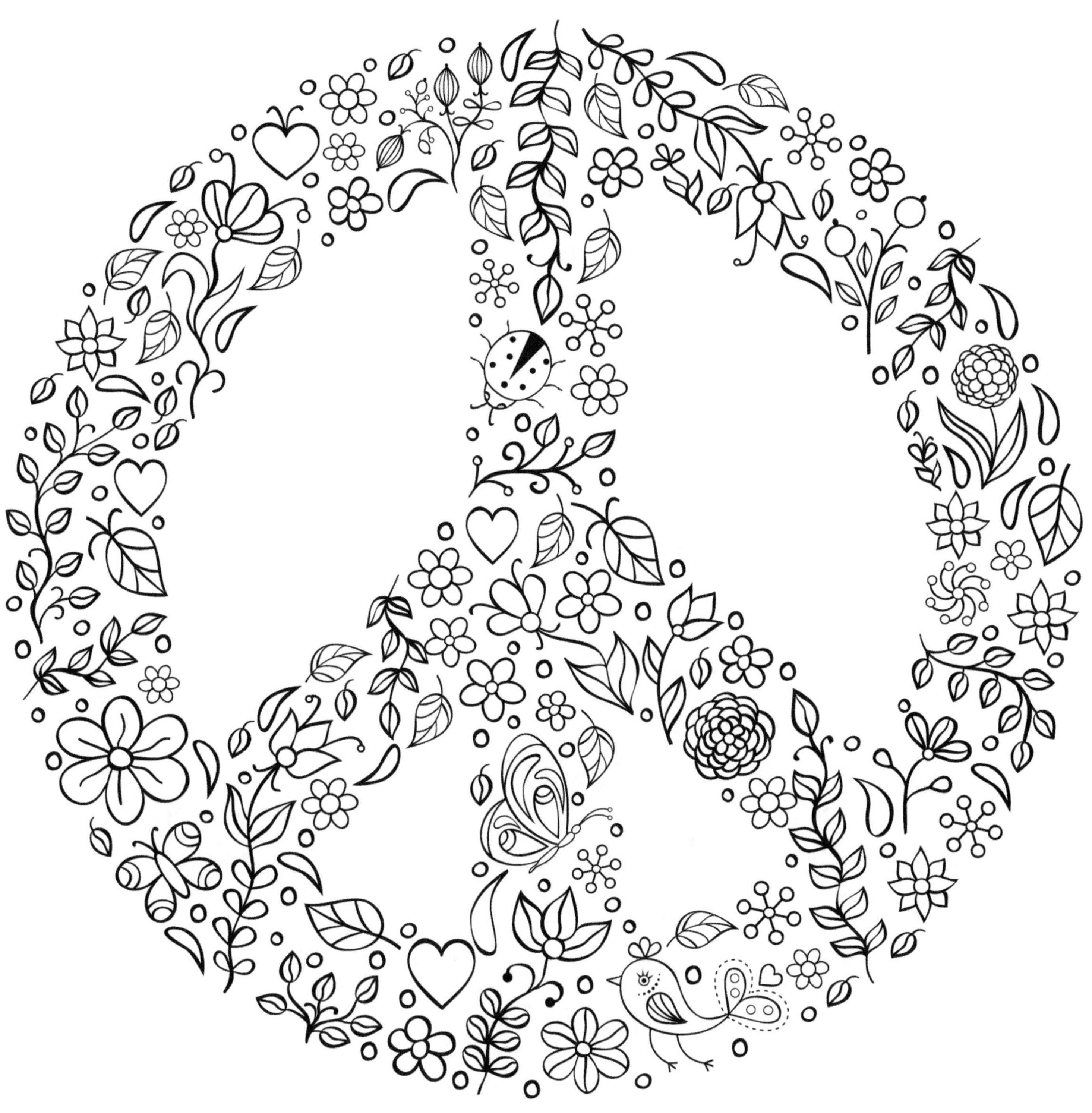

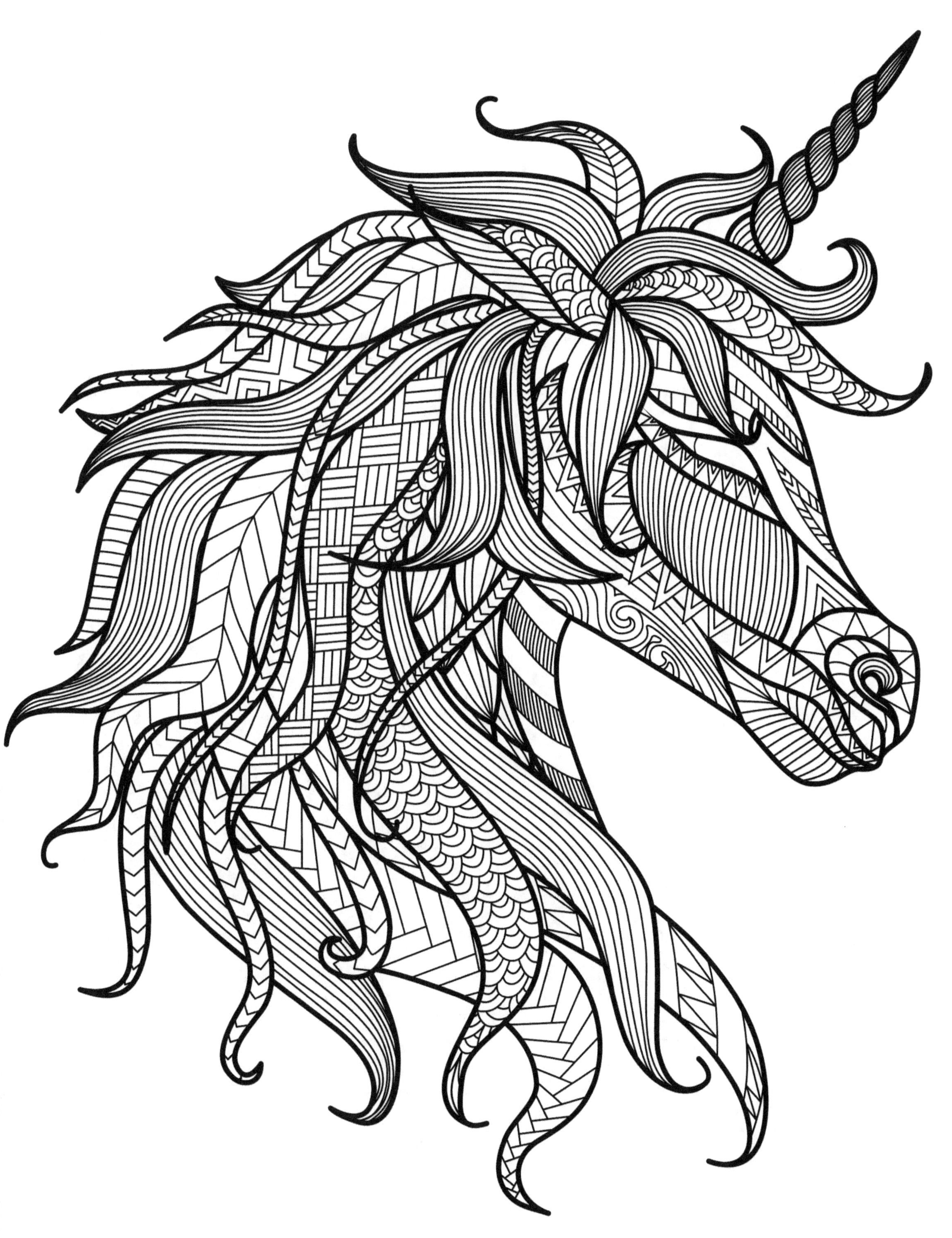

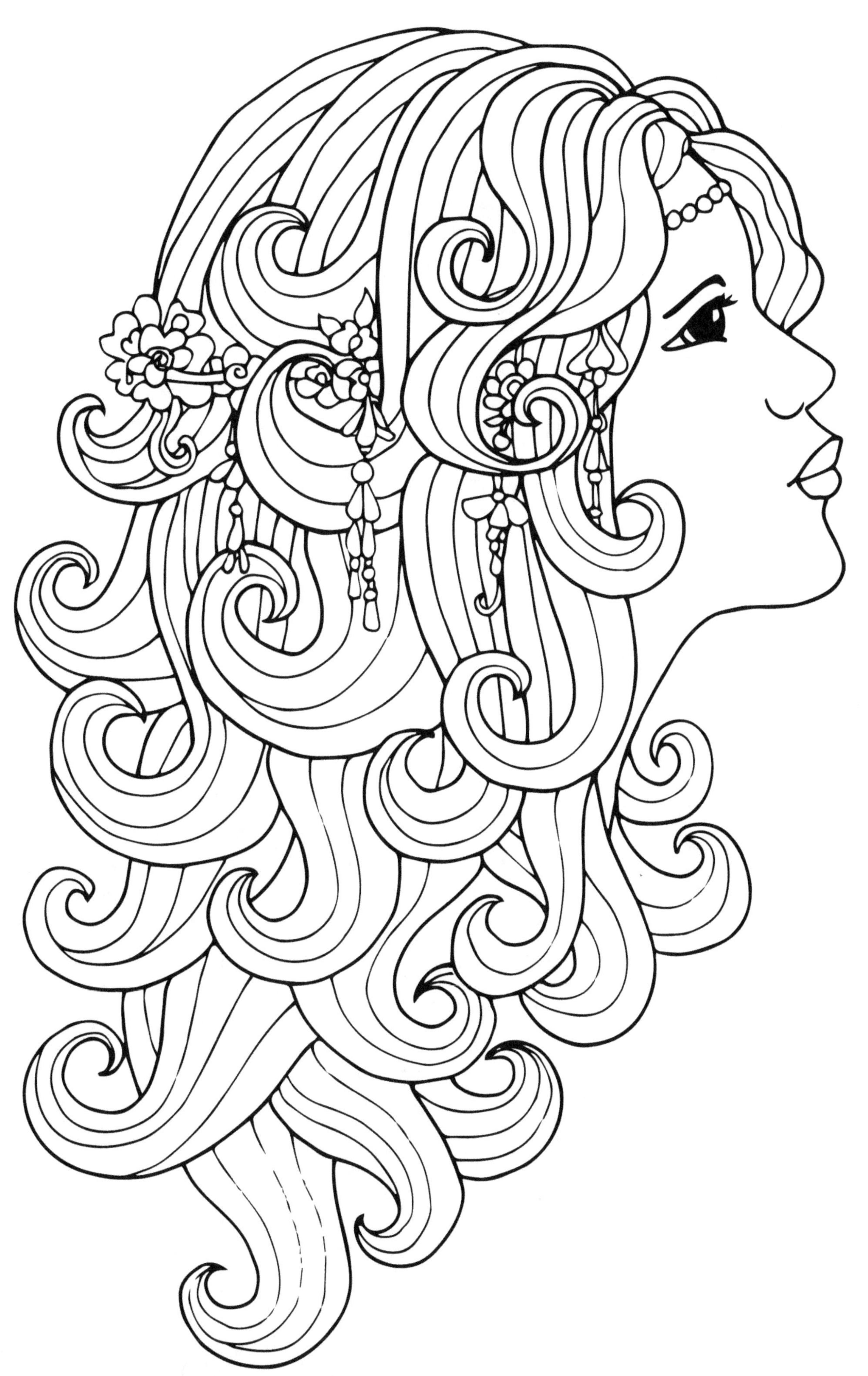

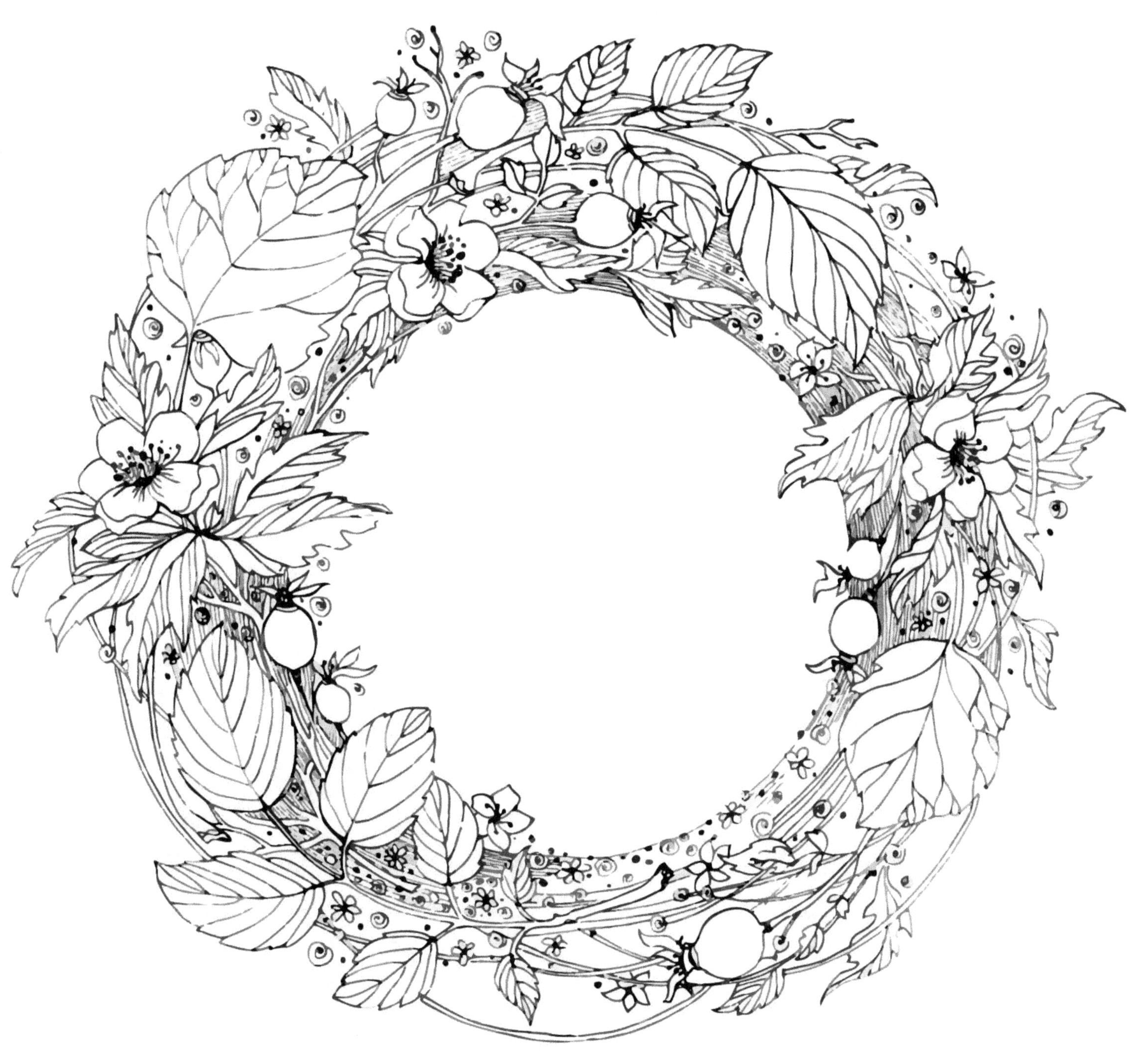

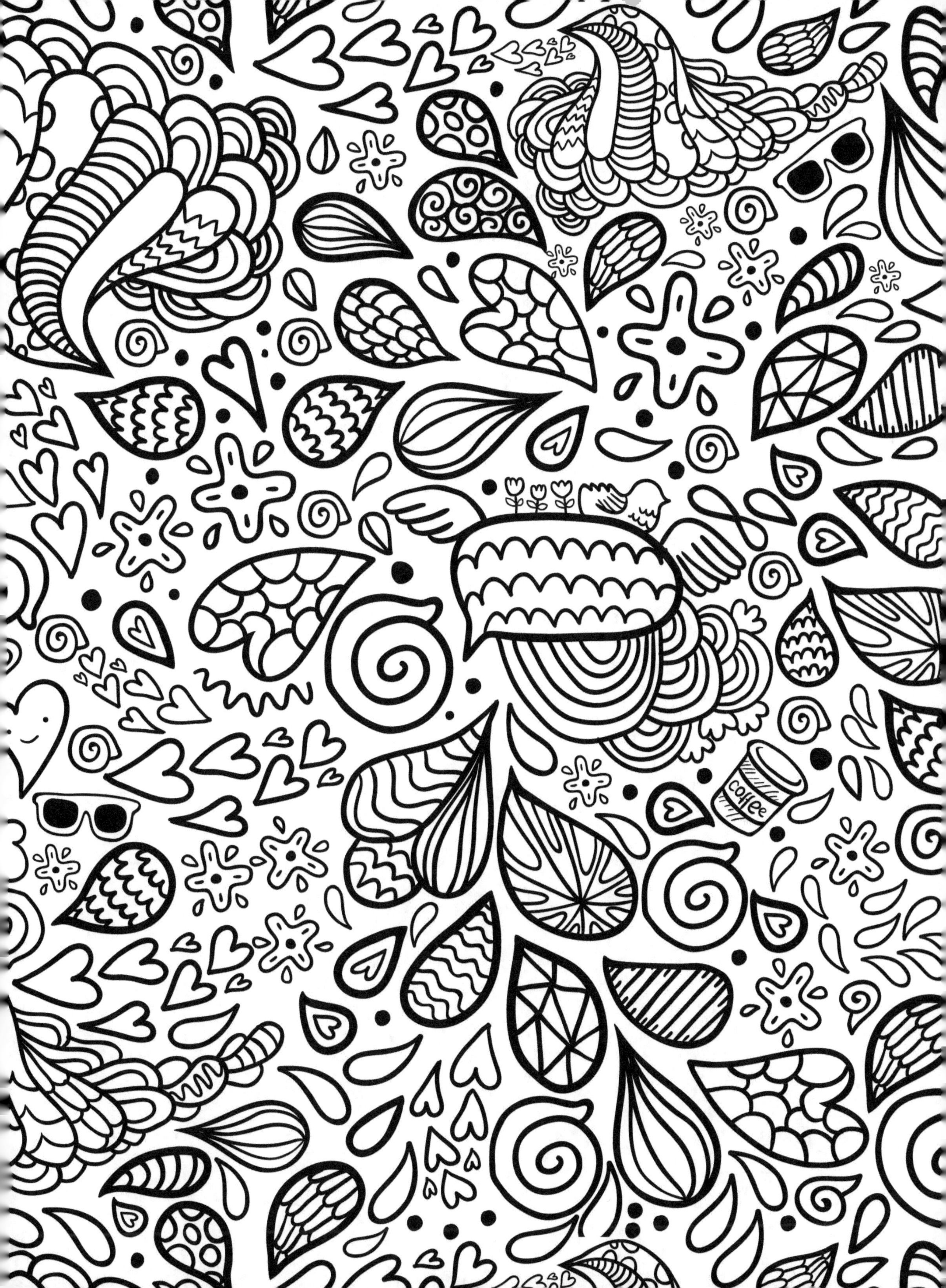
coffee

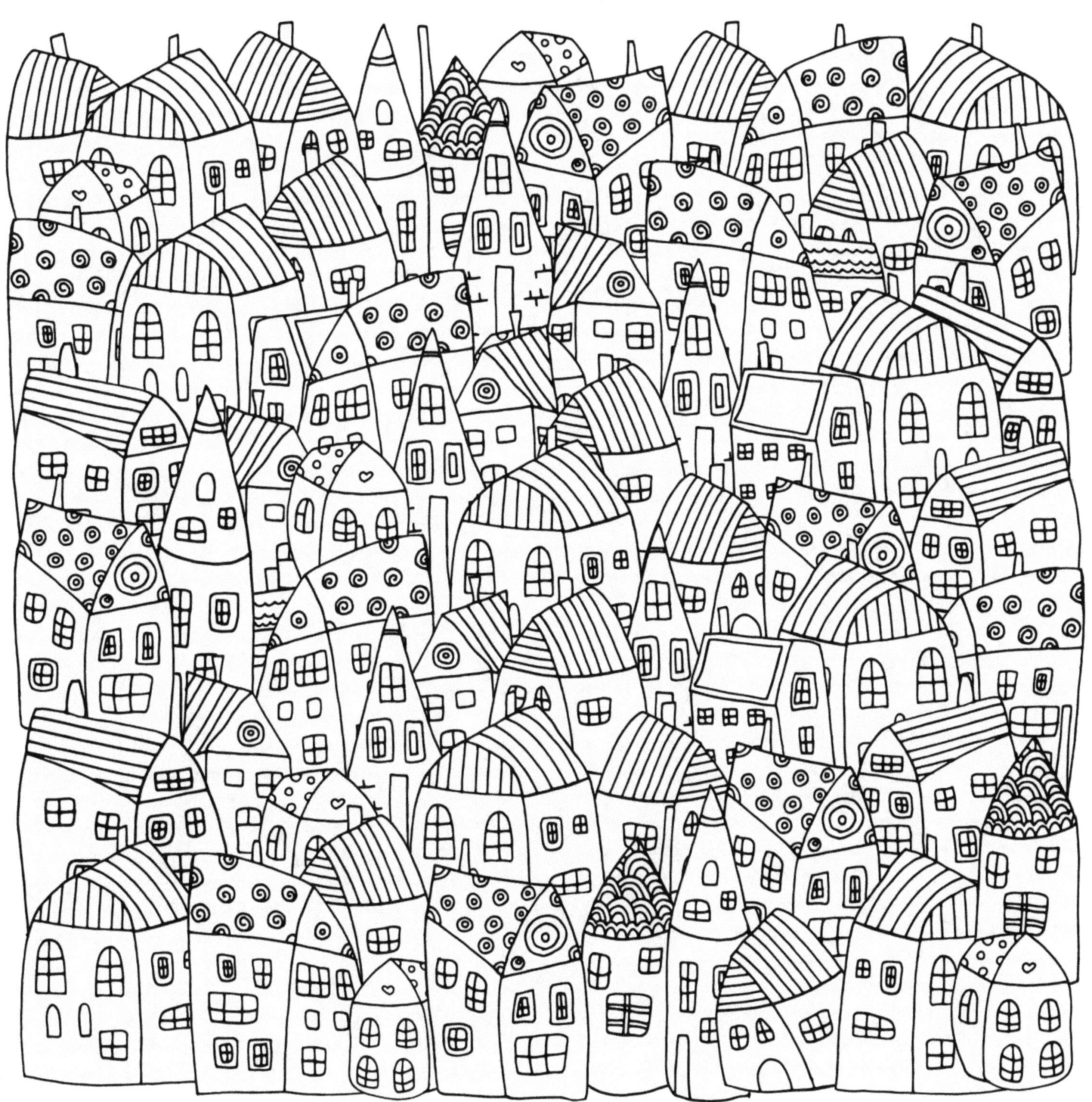

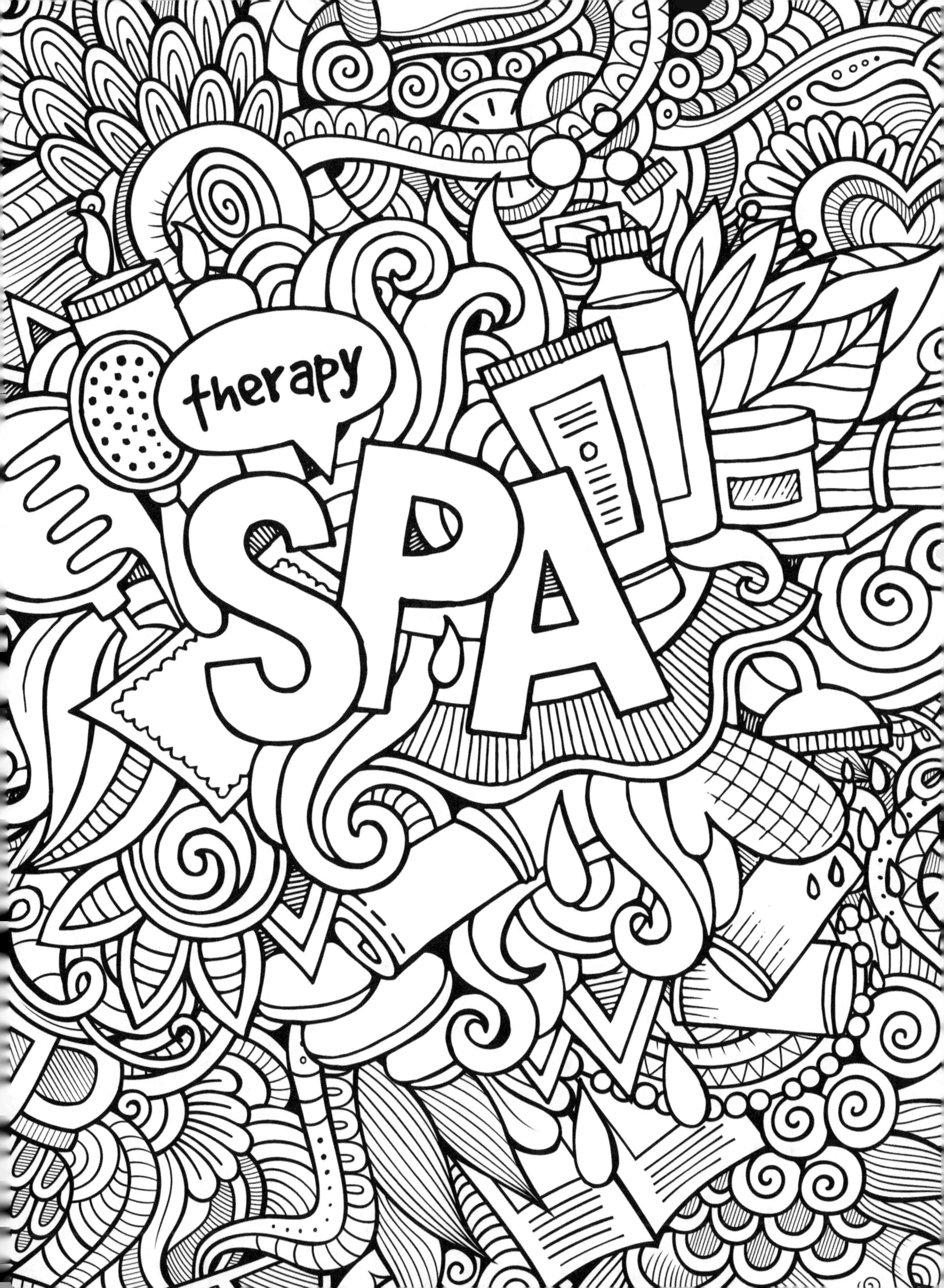
therapy
SPA!

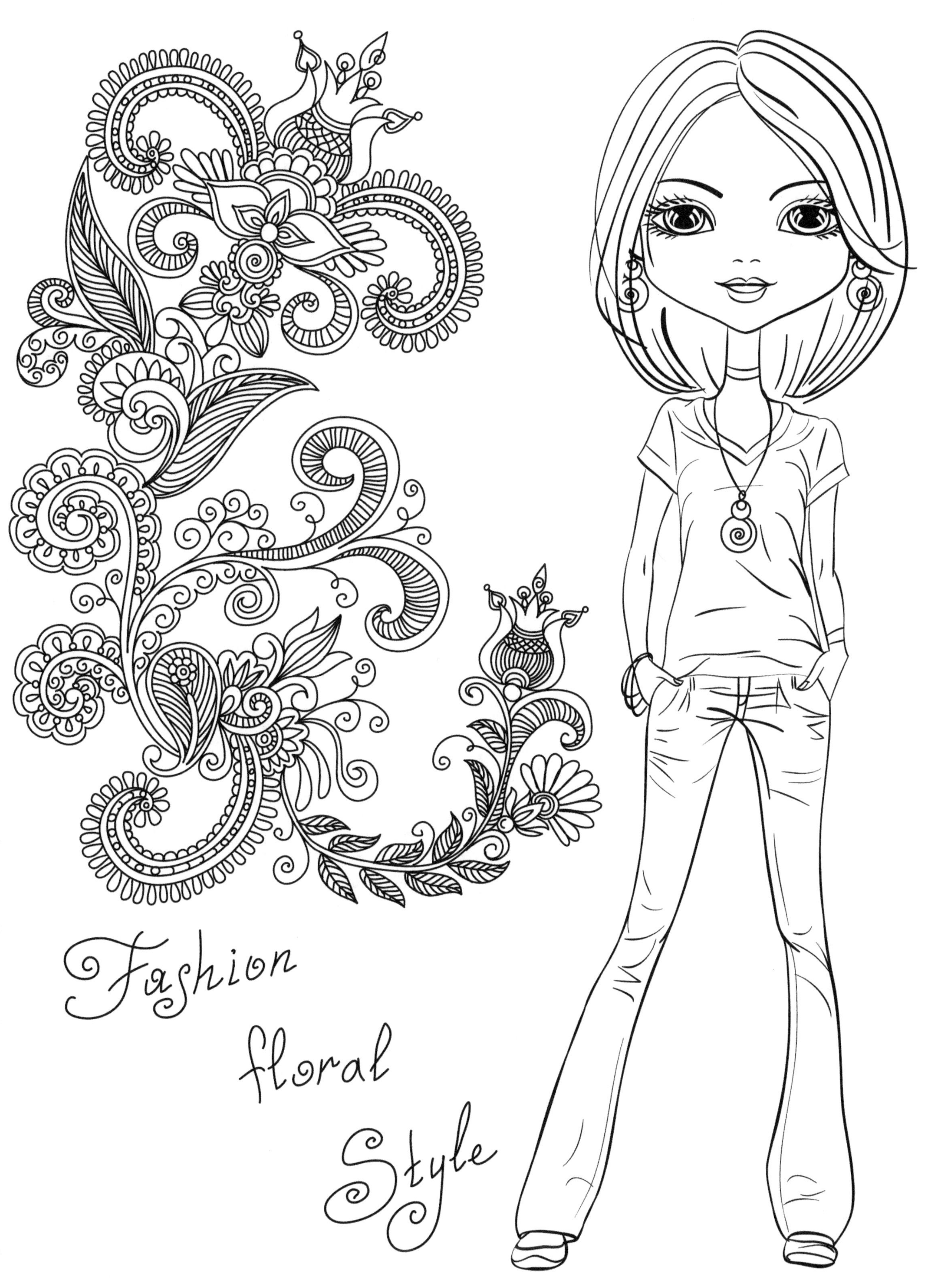
Fashion
floral
Style

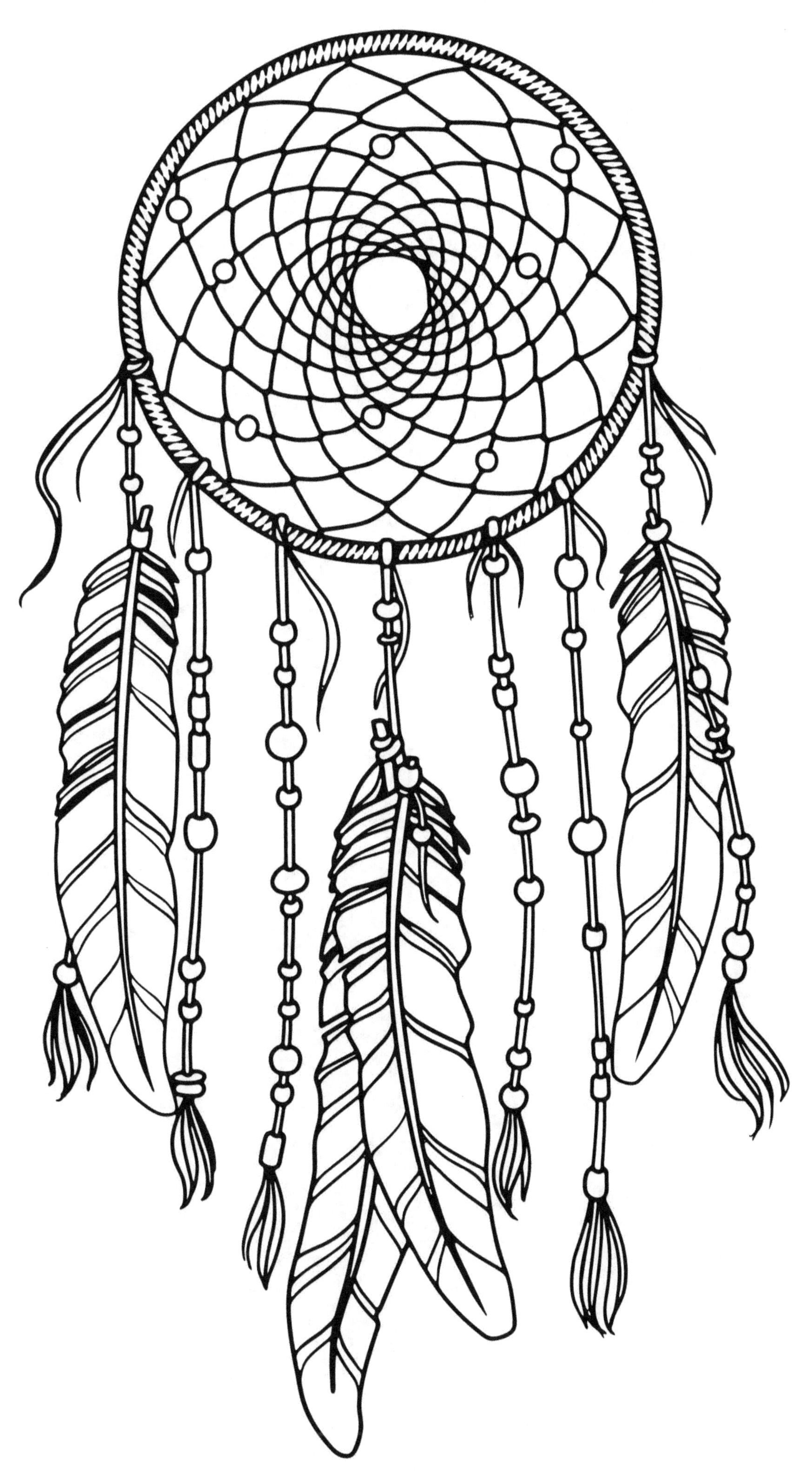

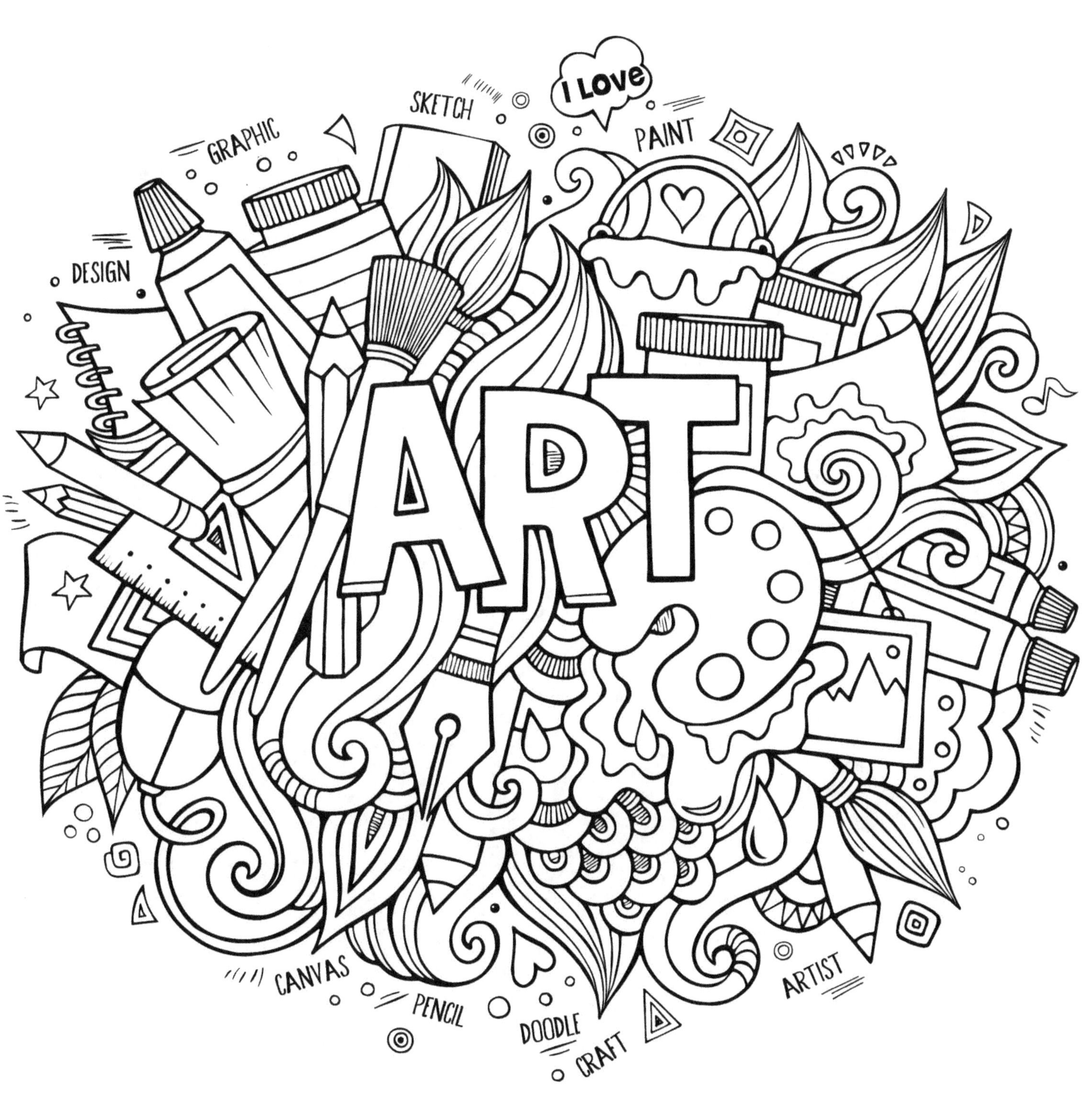
I Love
SKETCH
GRAPHIC
PAINT
DESIGN
ART
CANVAS
PENCIL
DOODLE
CRAFT
ARTIST

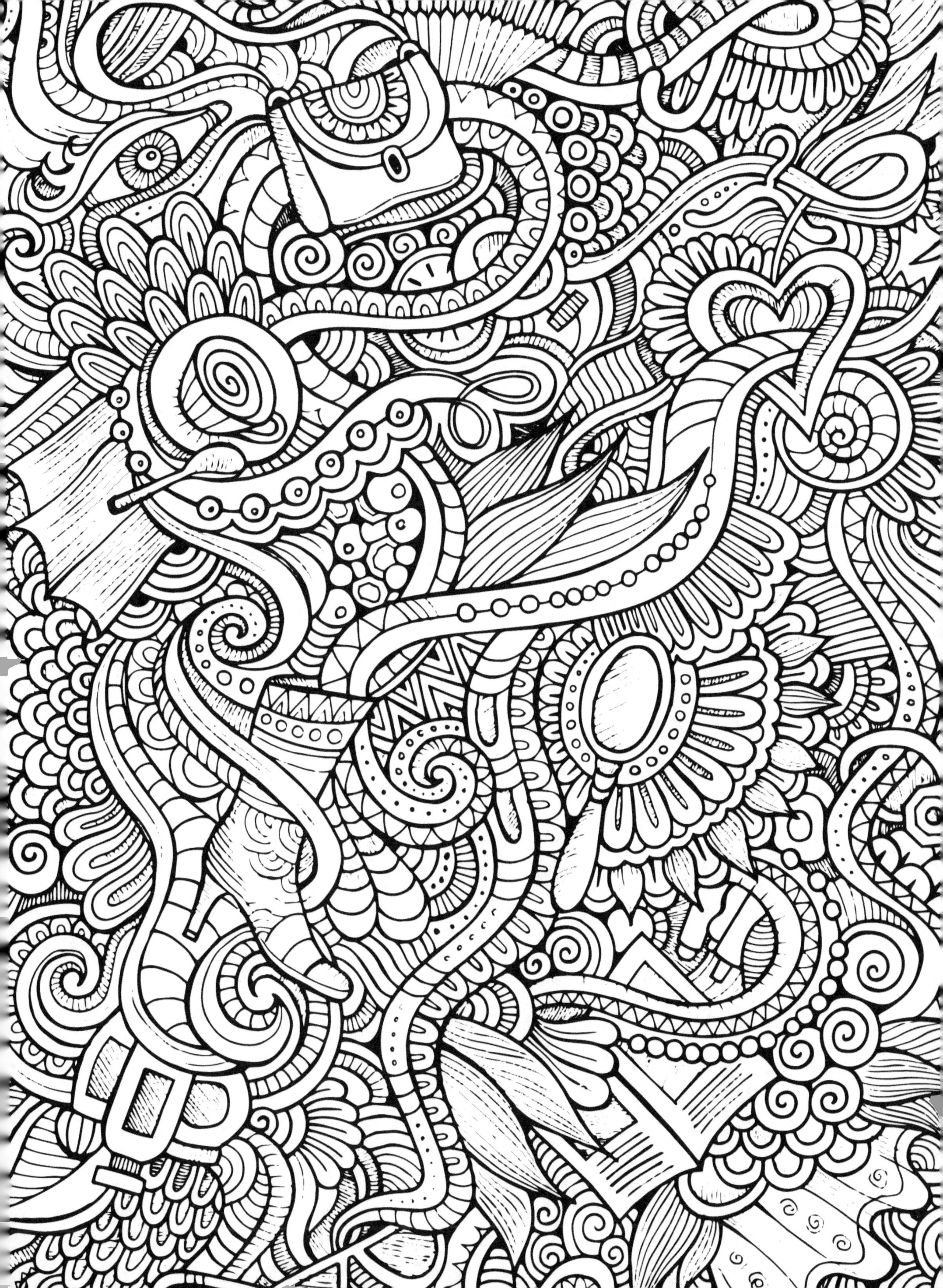

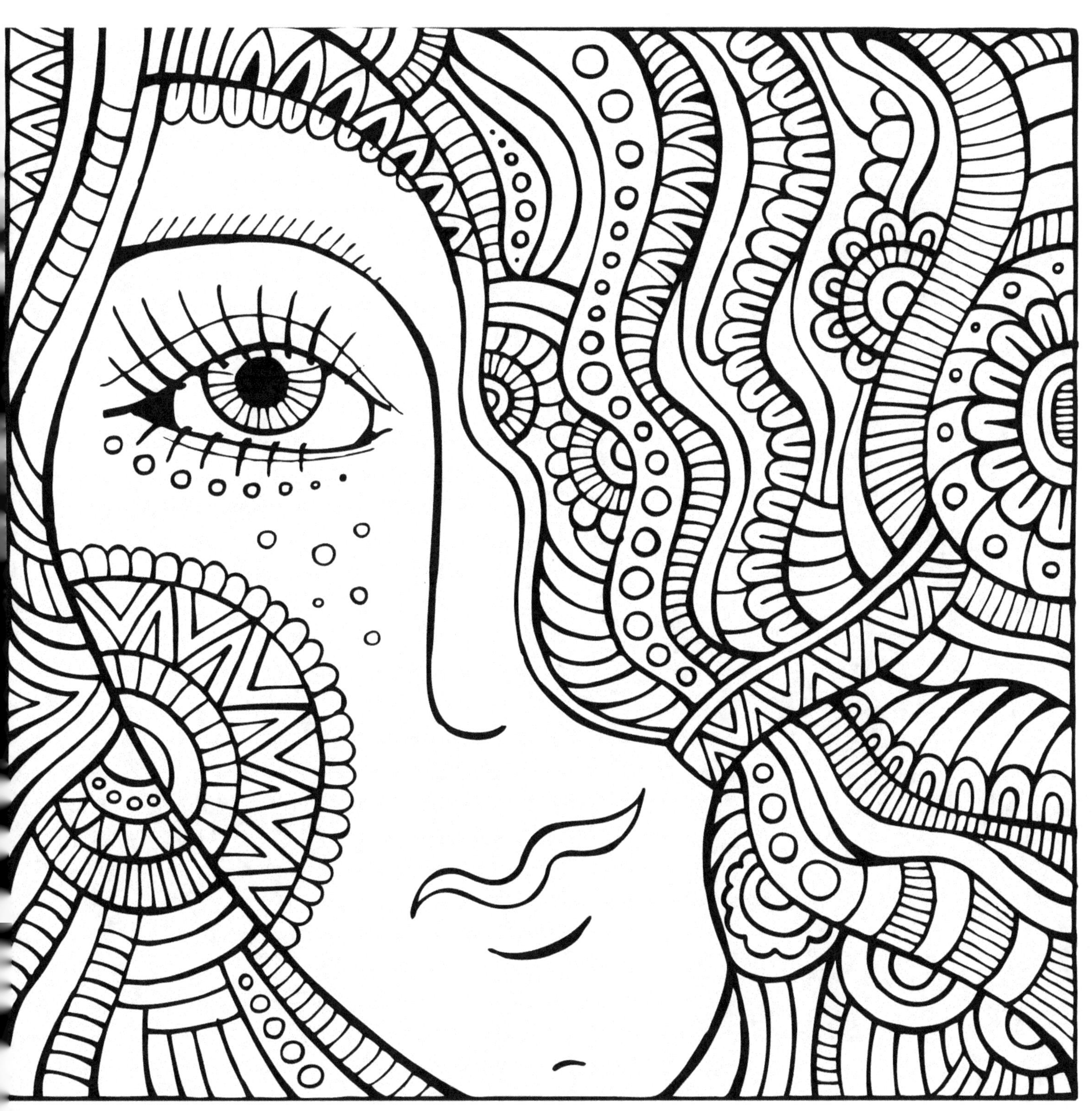

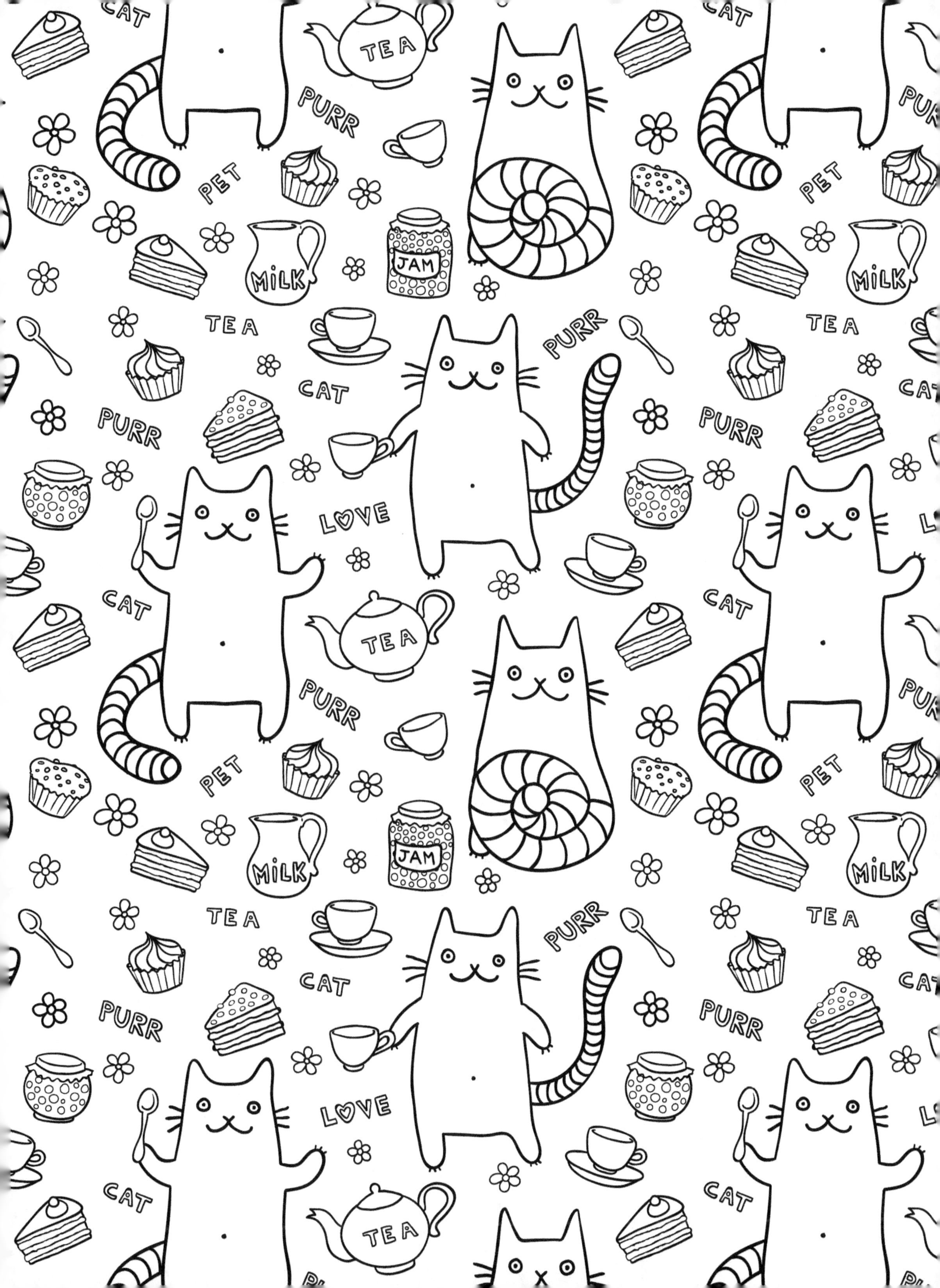

CAT
TEA
CAT
PURR
PET
PET
MILK
JAM
MILK
TEA
PURR
TEA
CAT
PURR
PURR
LOVE
CAT
TEA
CAT
PURR
PET
PET
MILK
JAM
MILK
TEA
PURR
TEA
CAT
PURR
PURR
LOVE
CAT
TEA
CAT

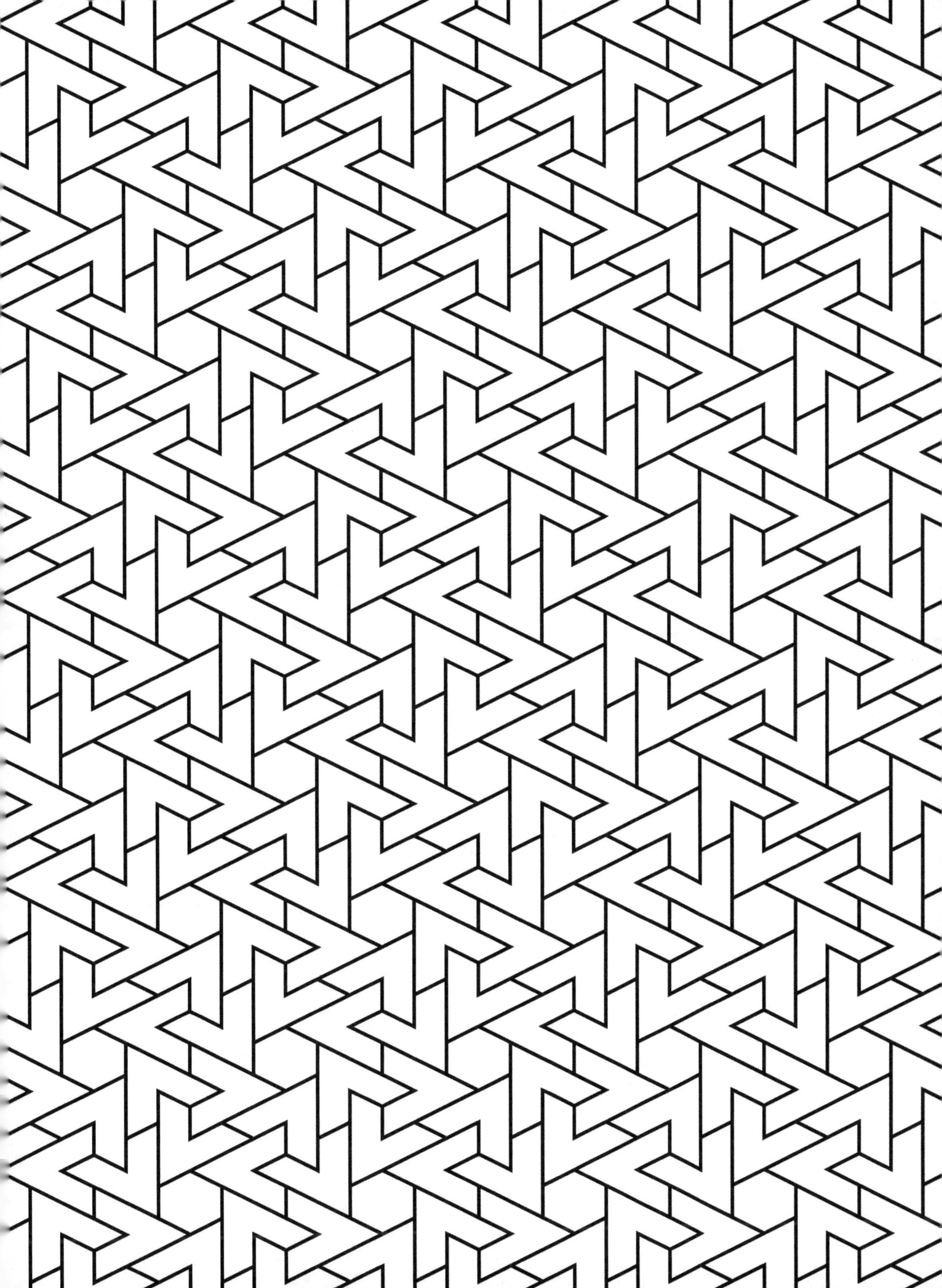

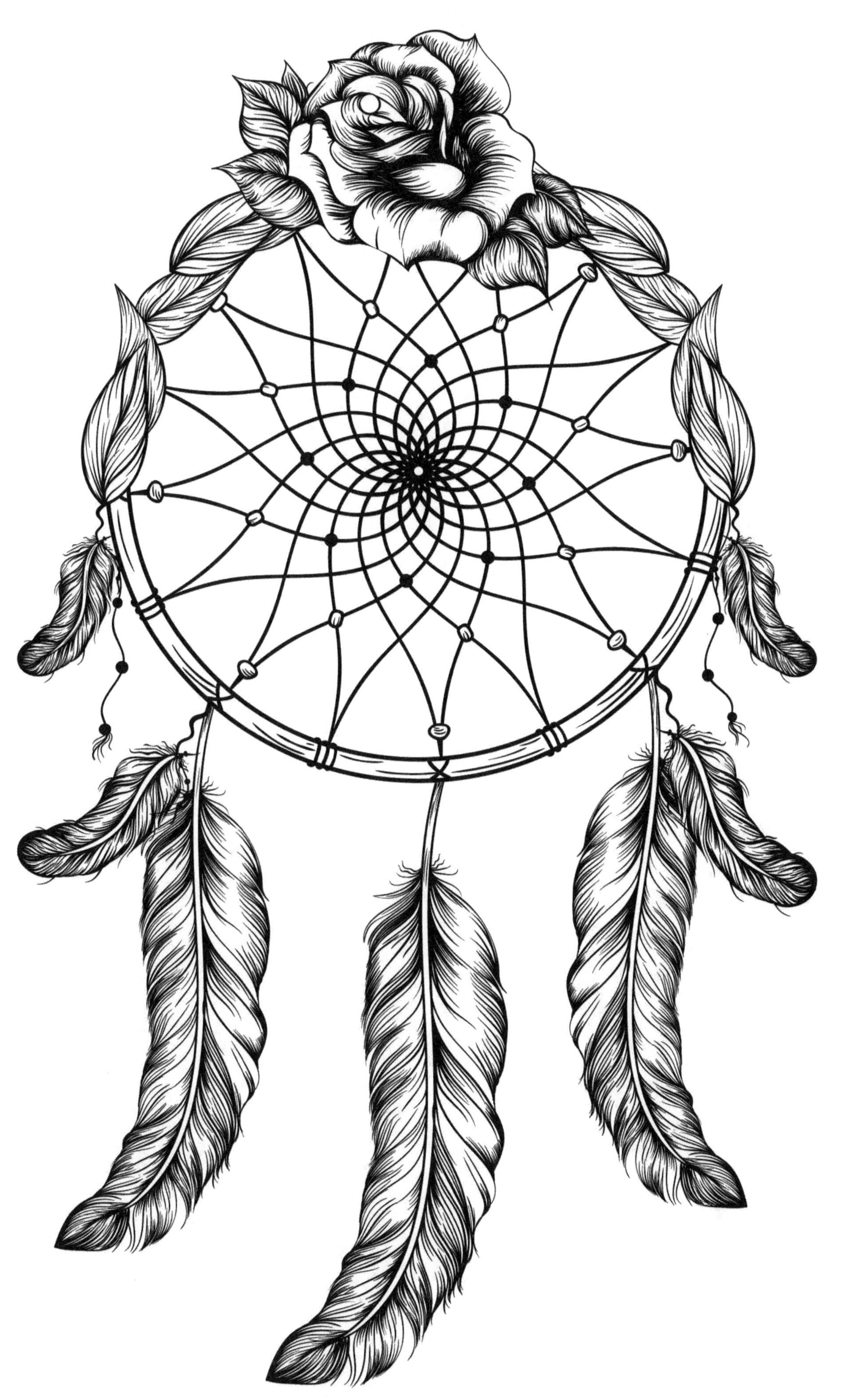

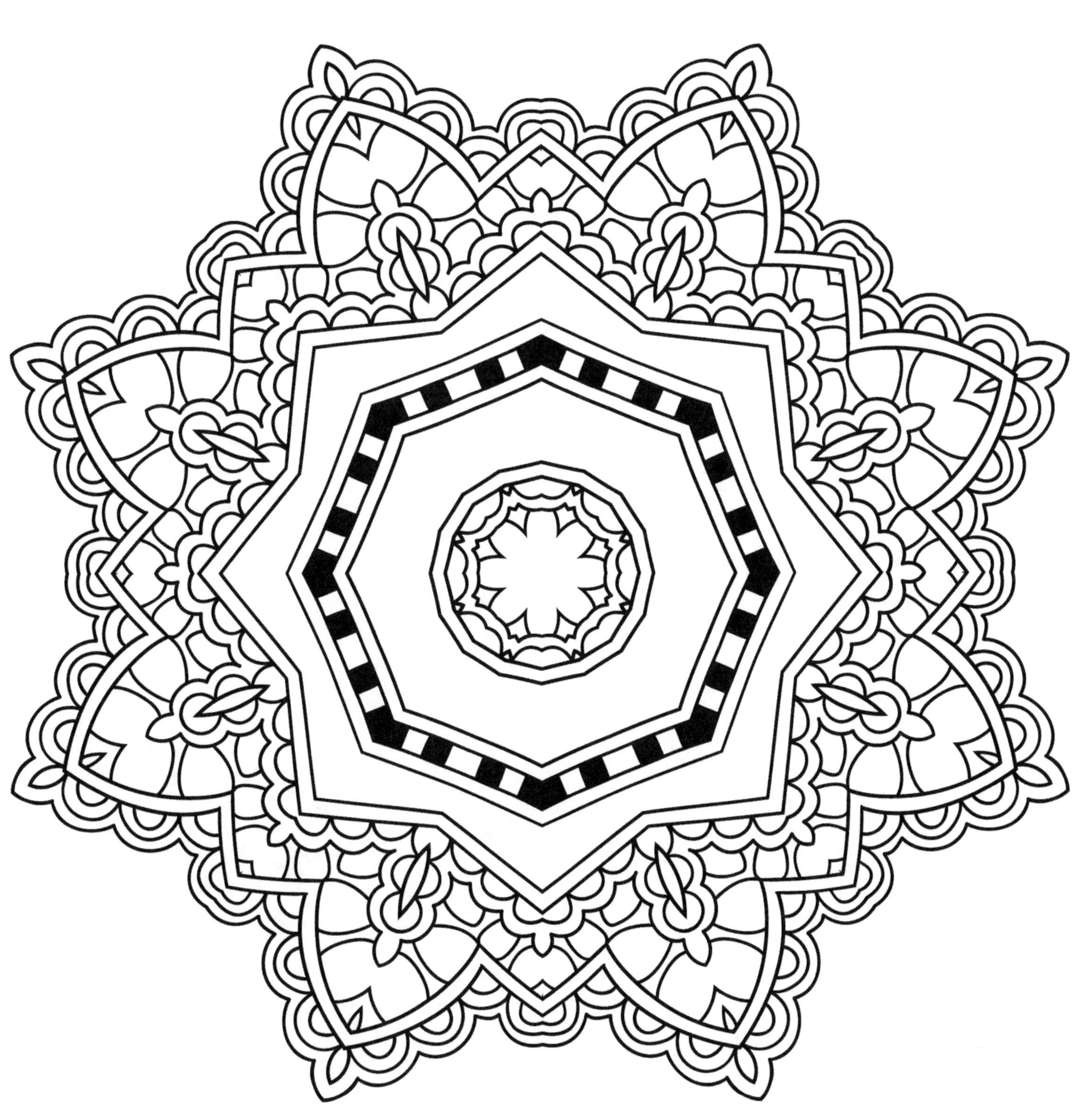

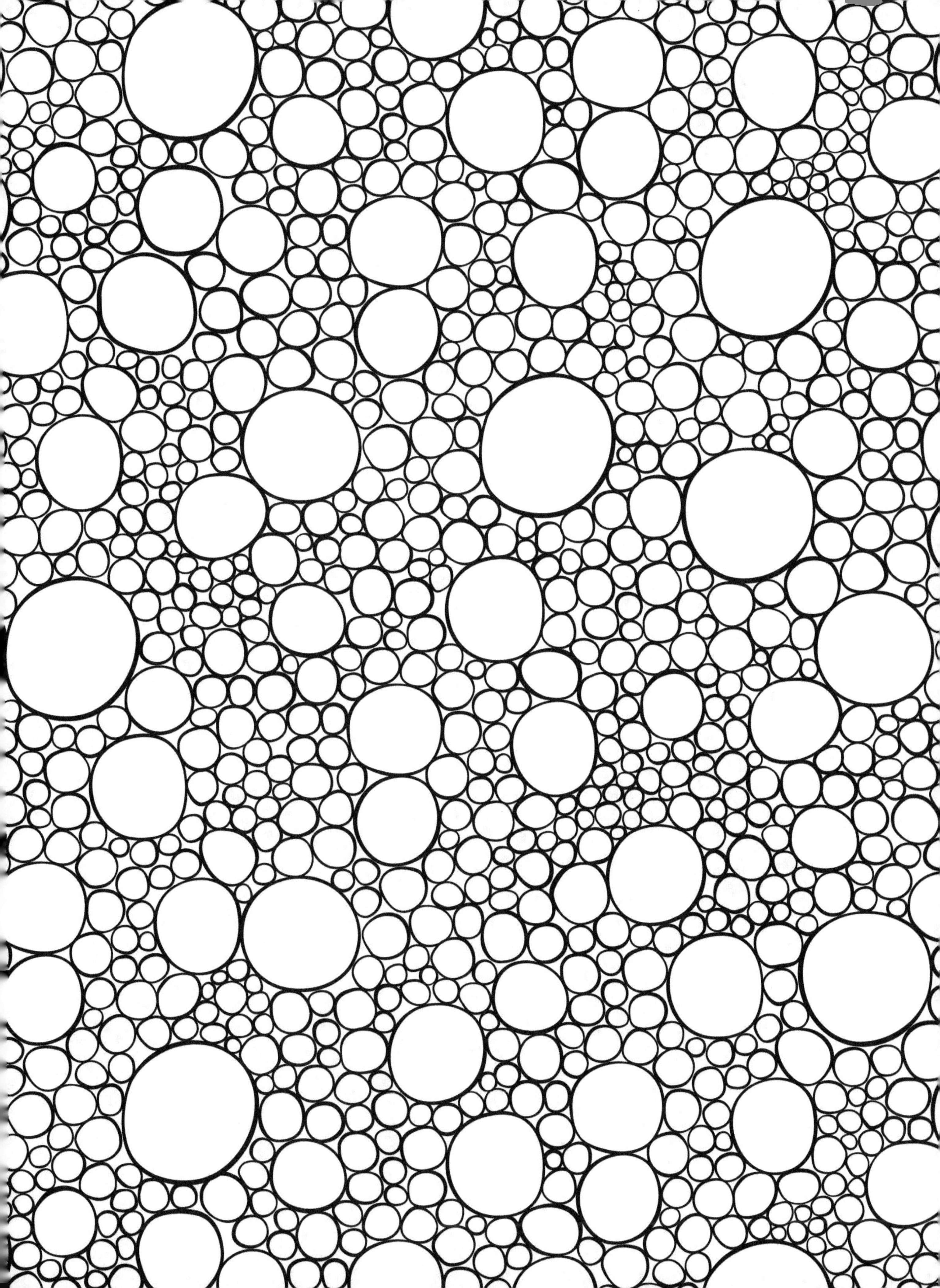

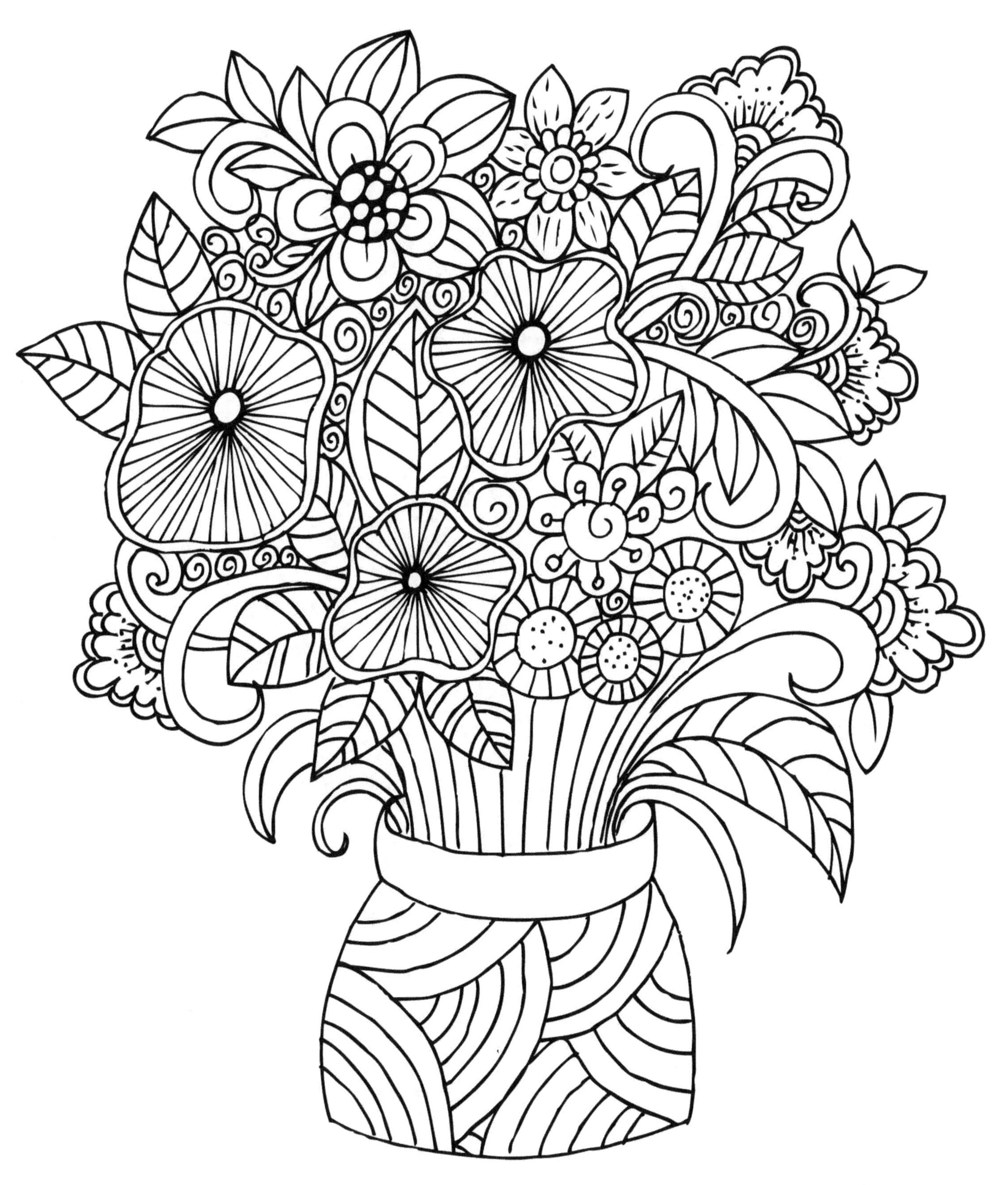

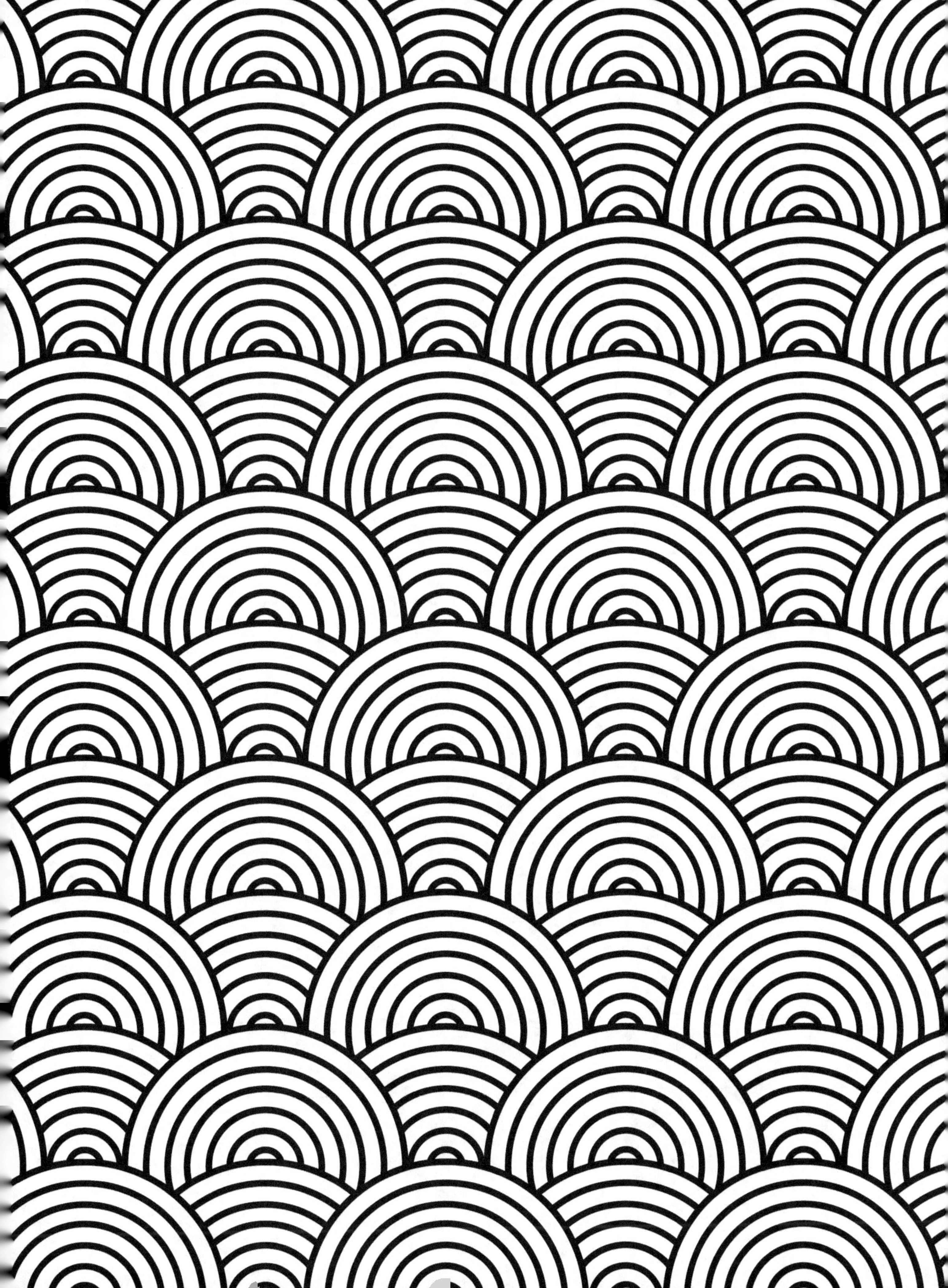

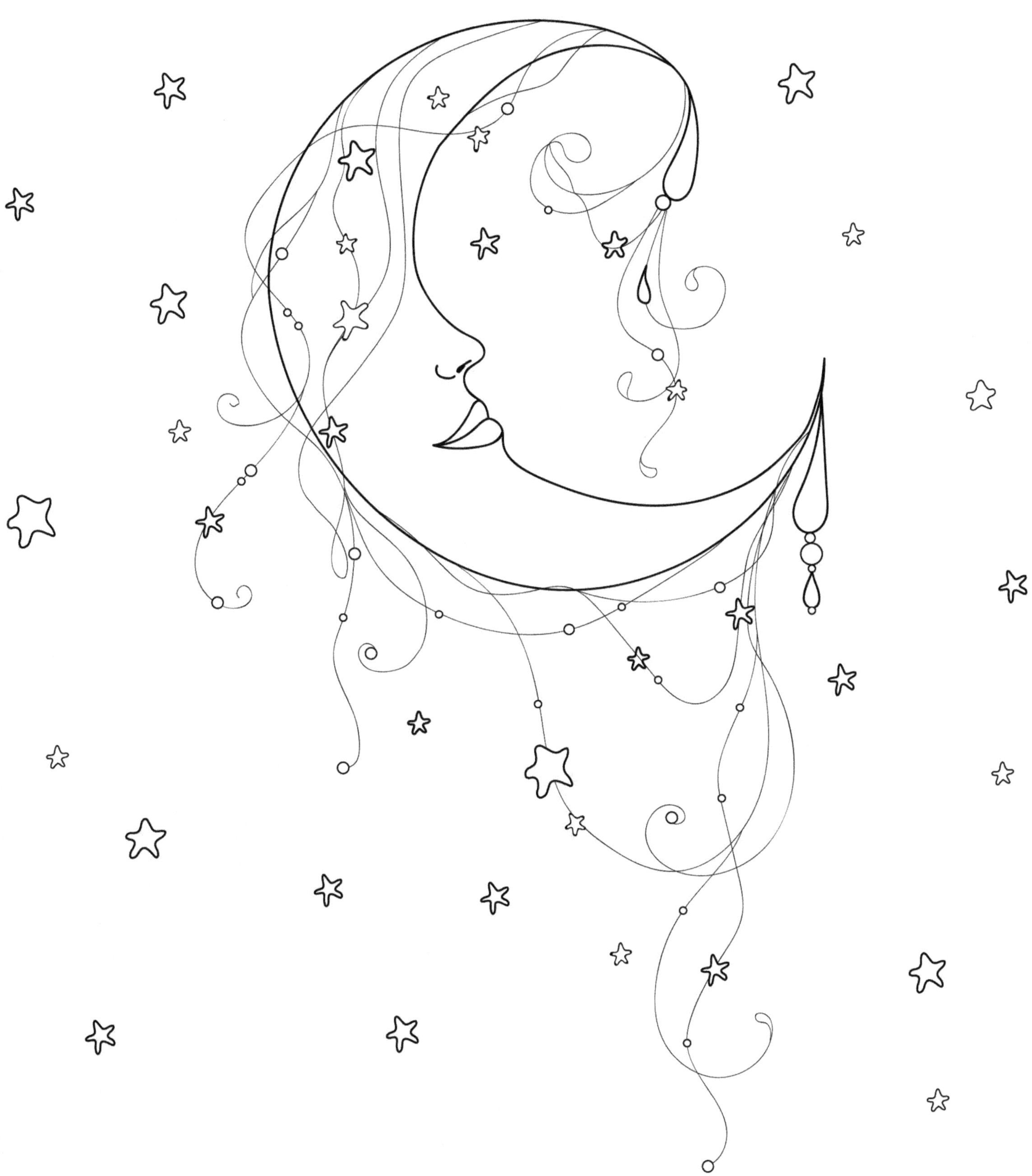

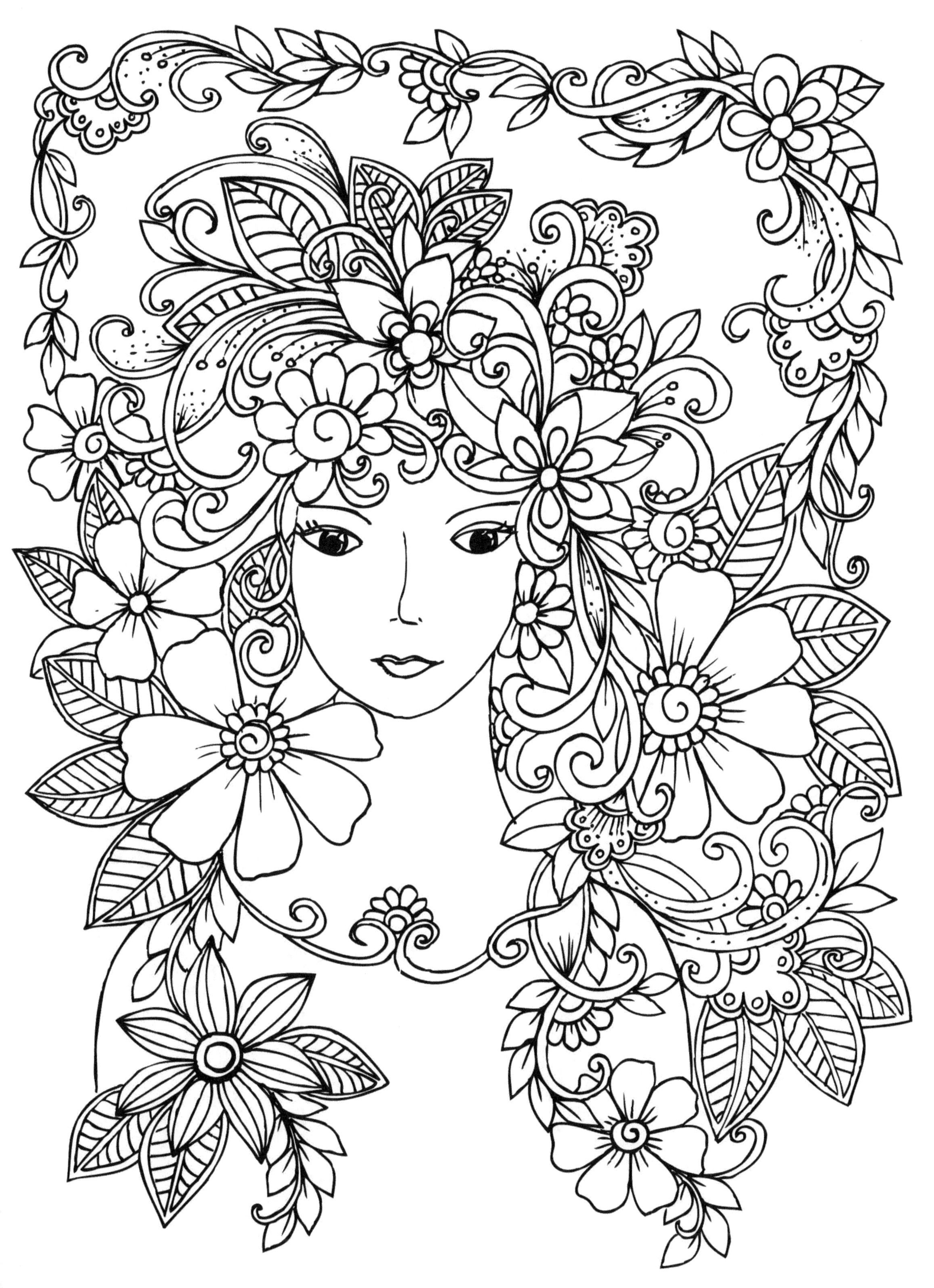

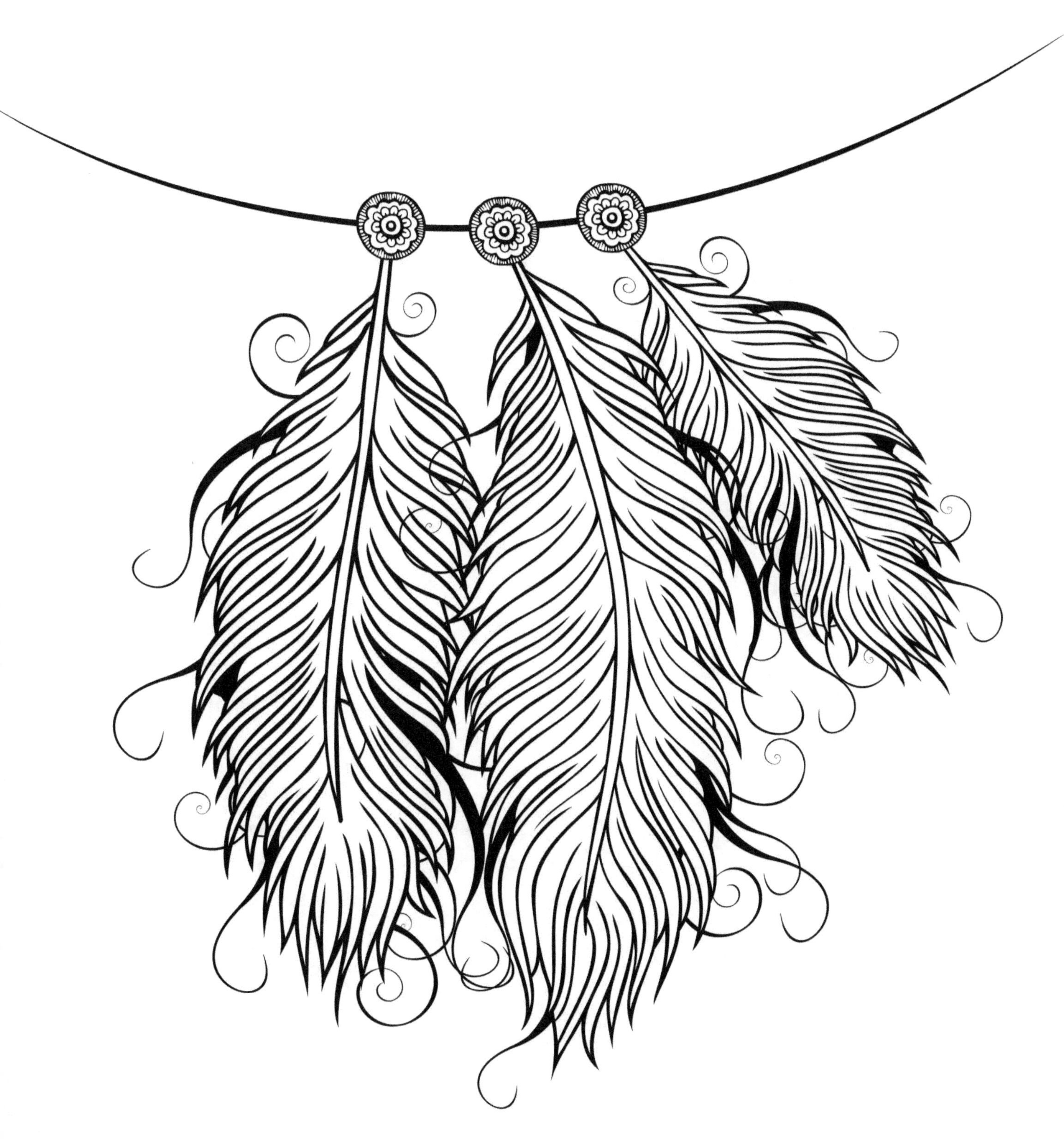

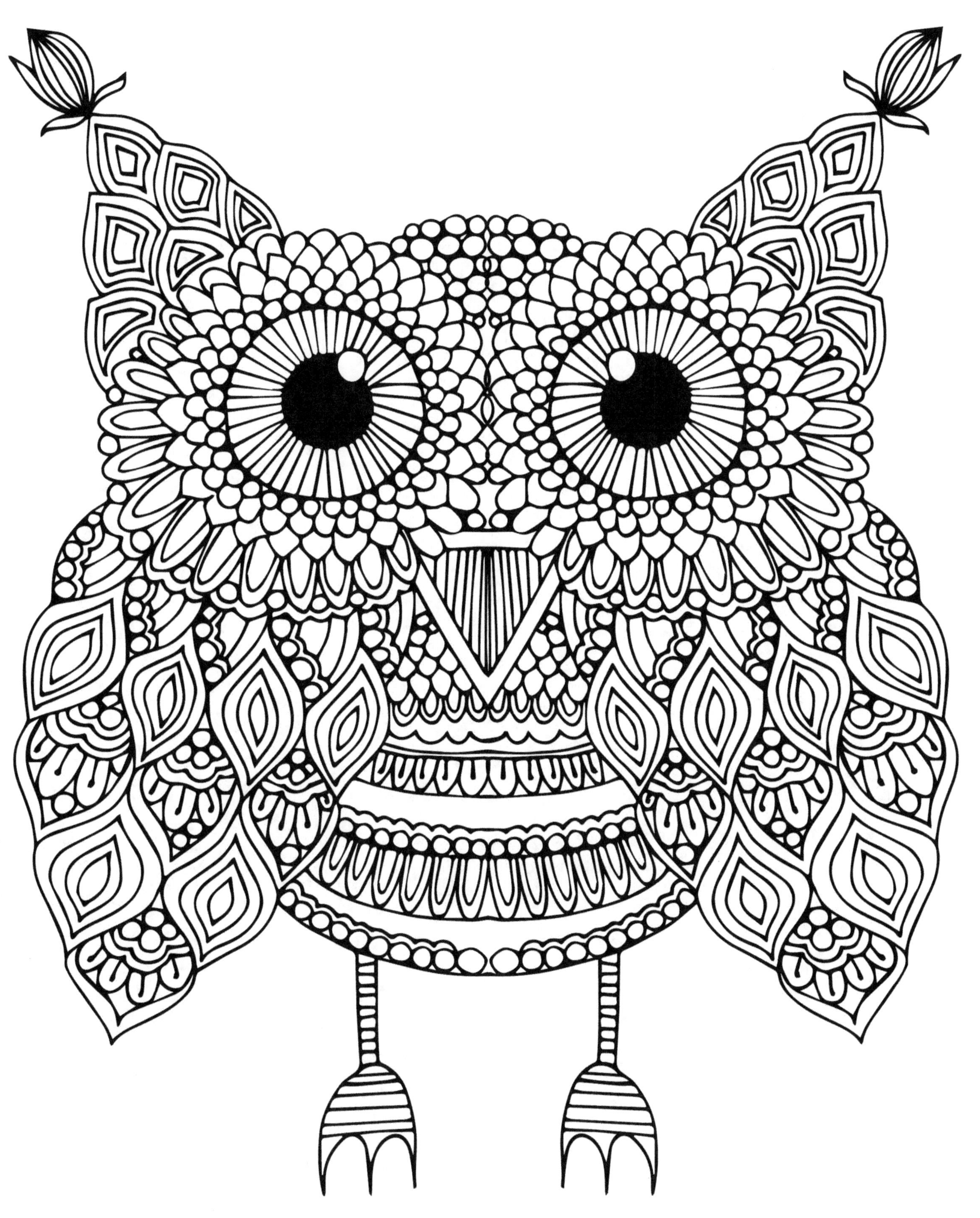

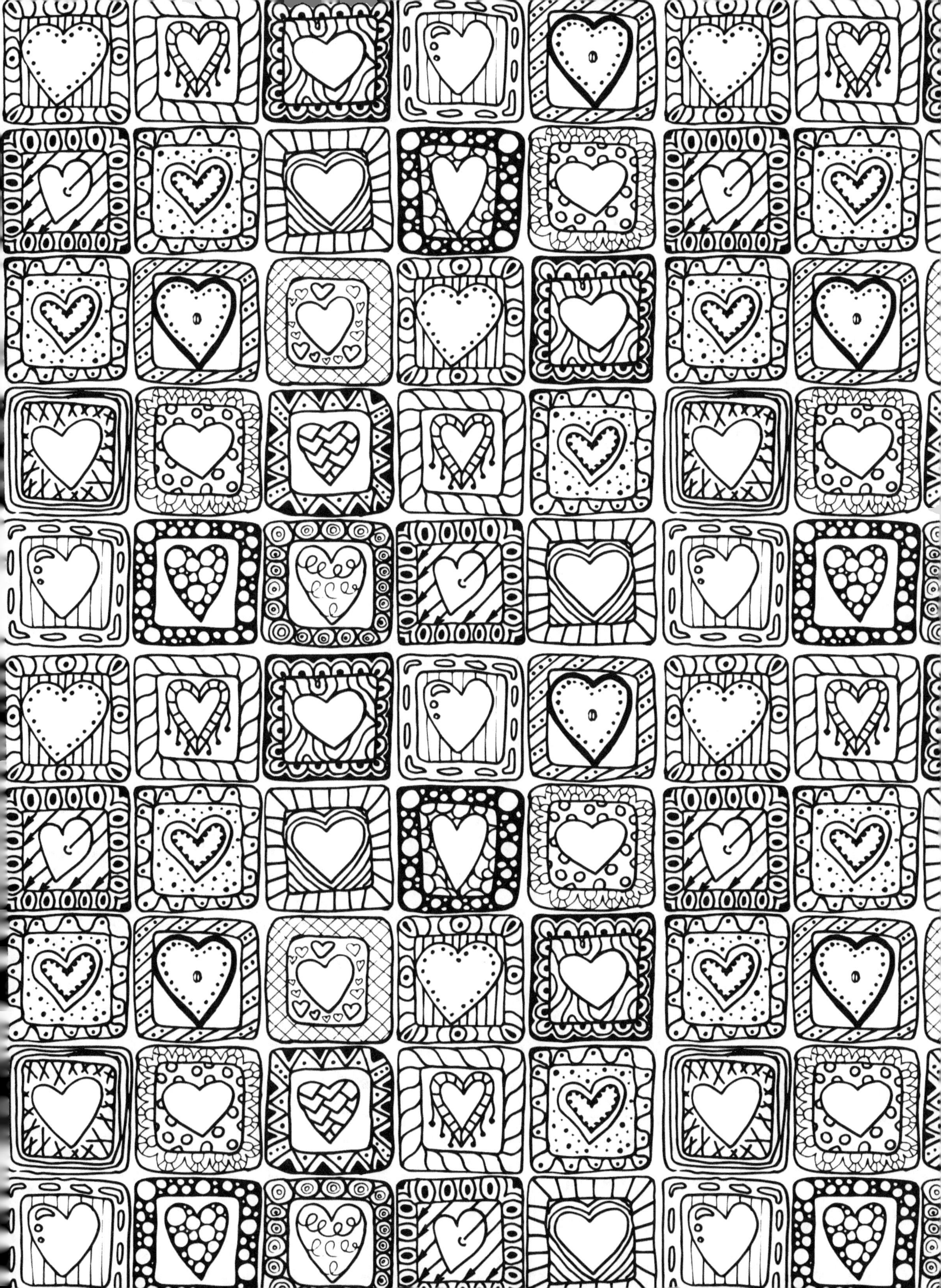

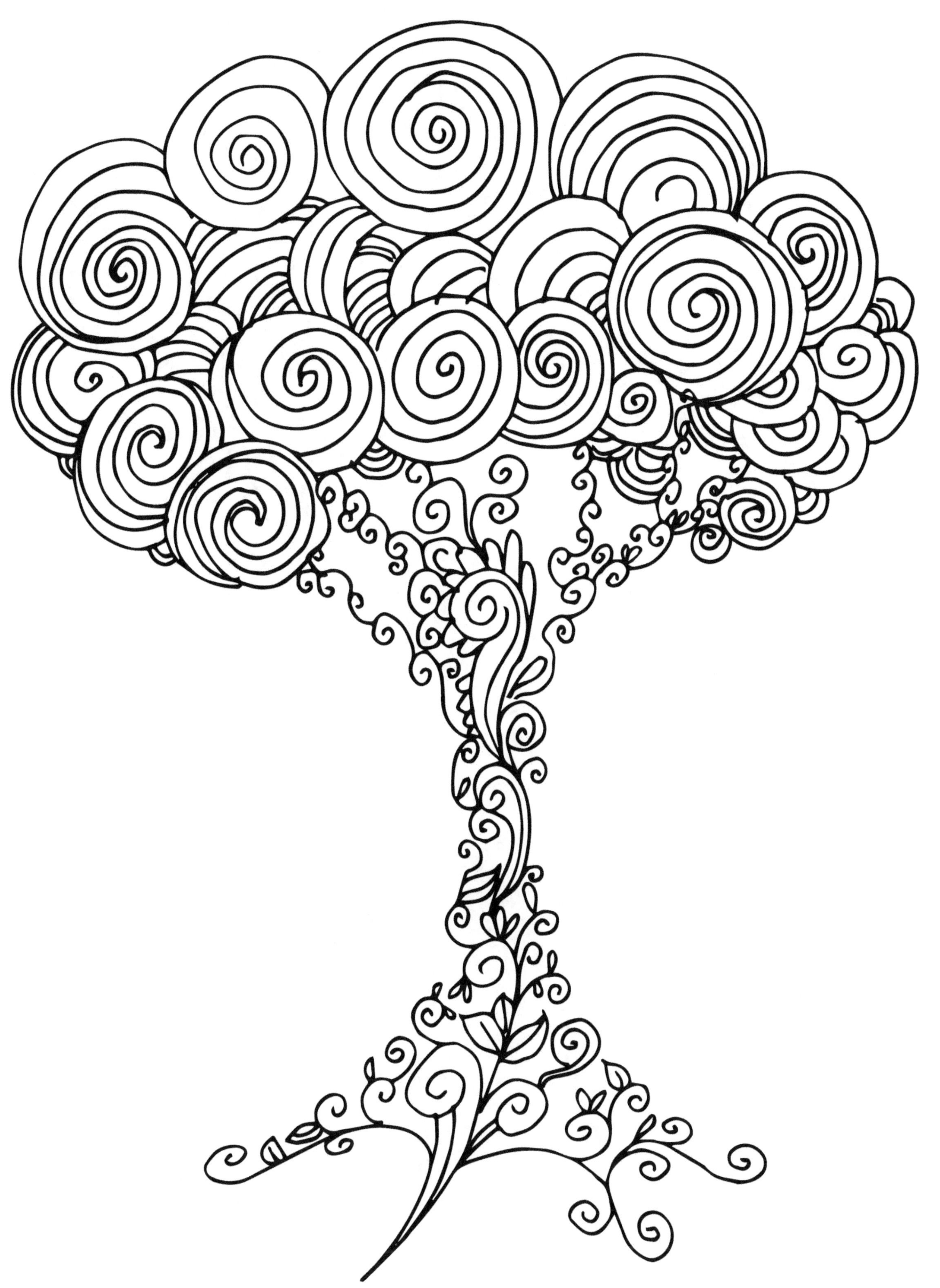

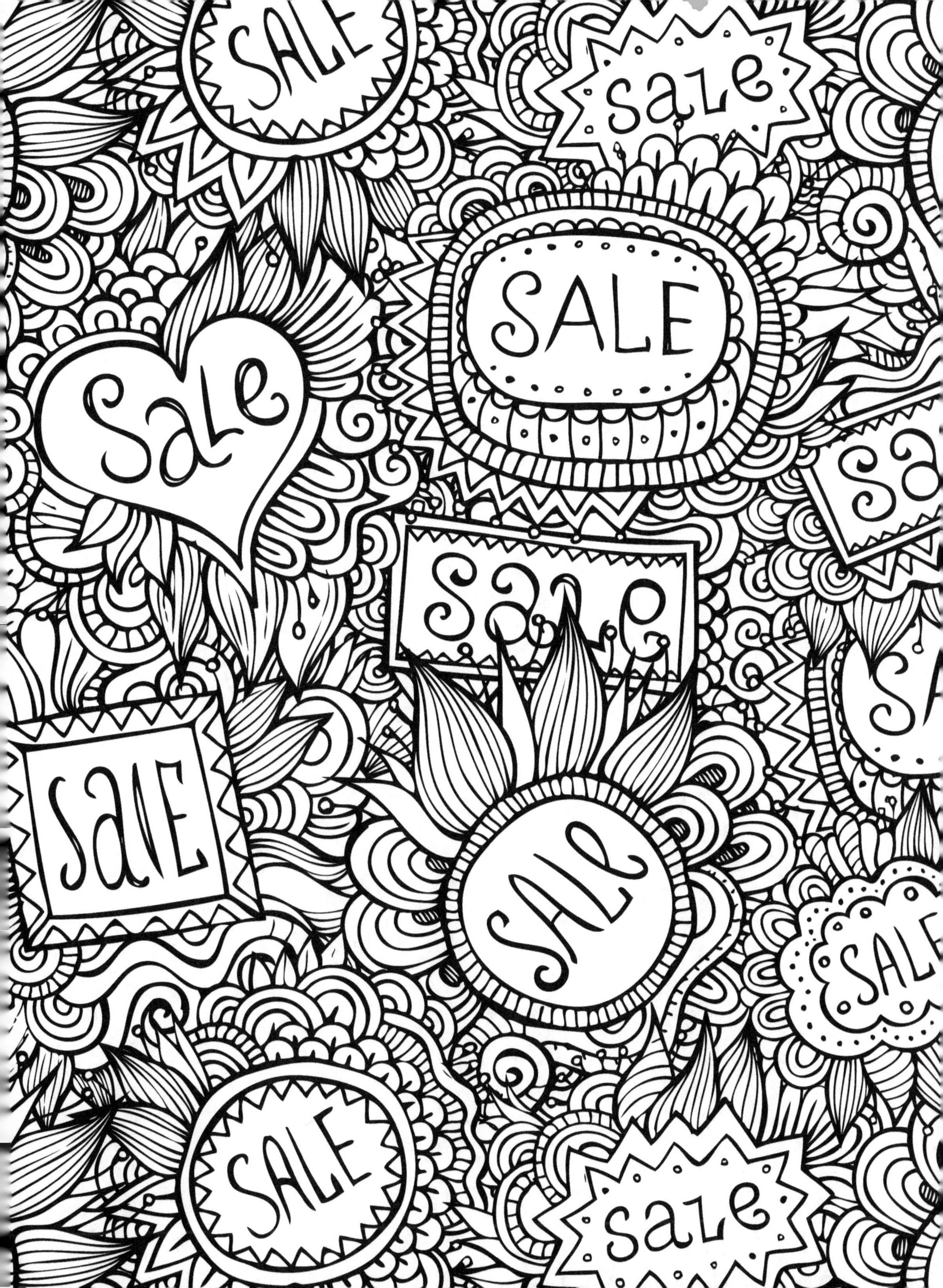
SALE
sale
SALE
Sale
sale
SALE
SALE
SALE
sale

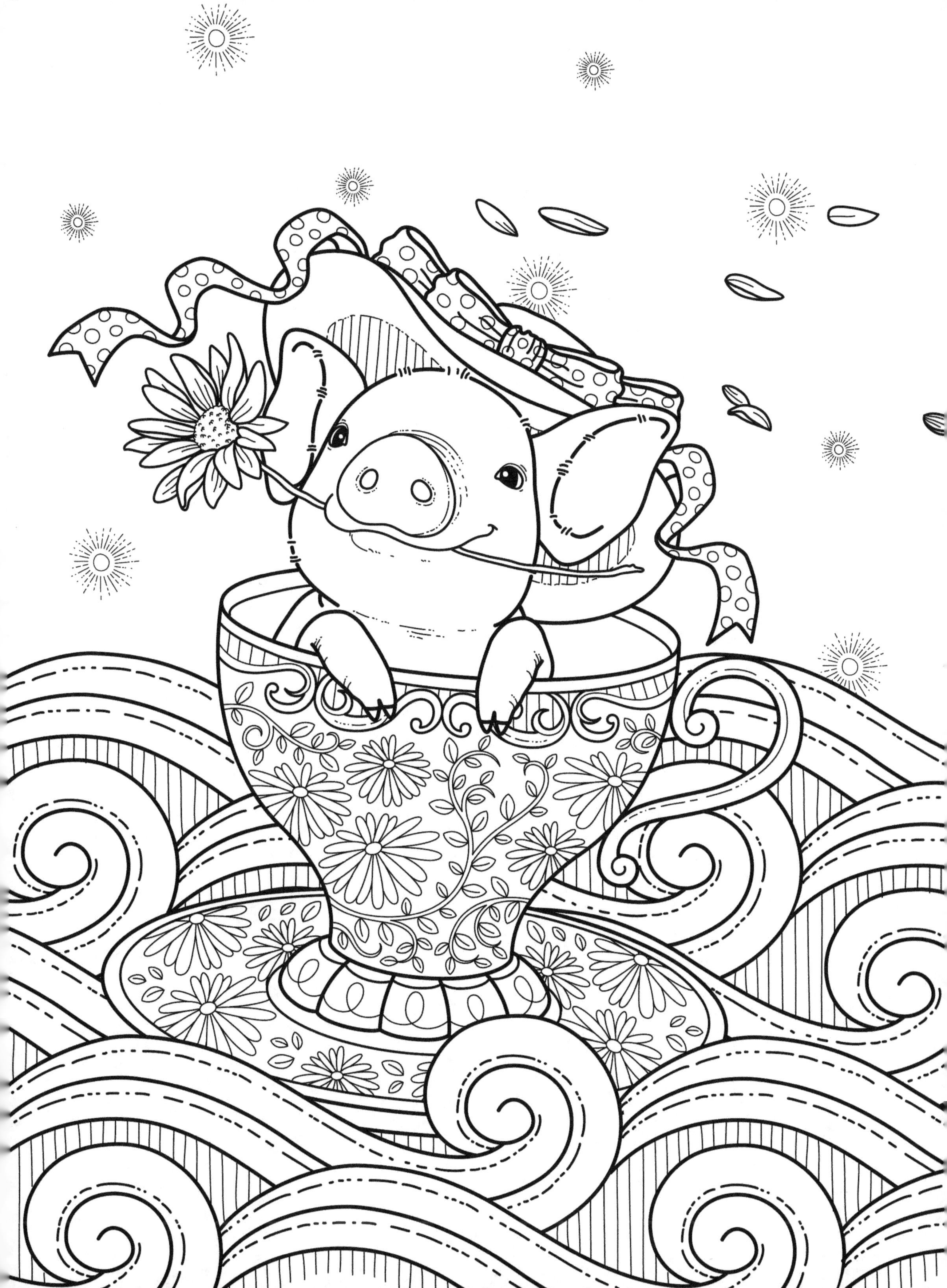

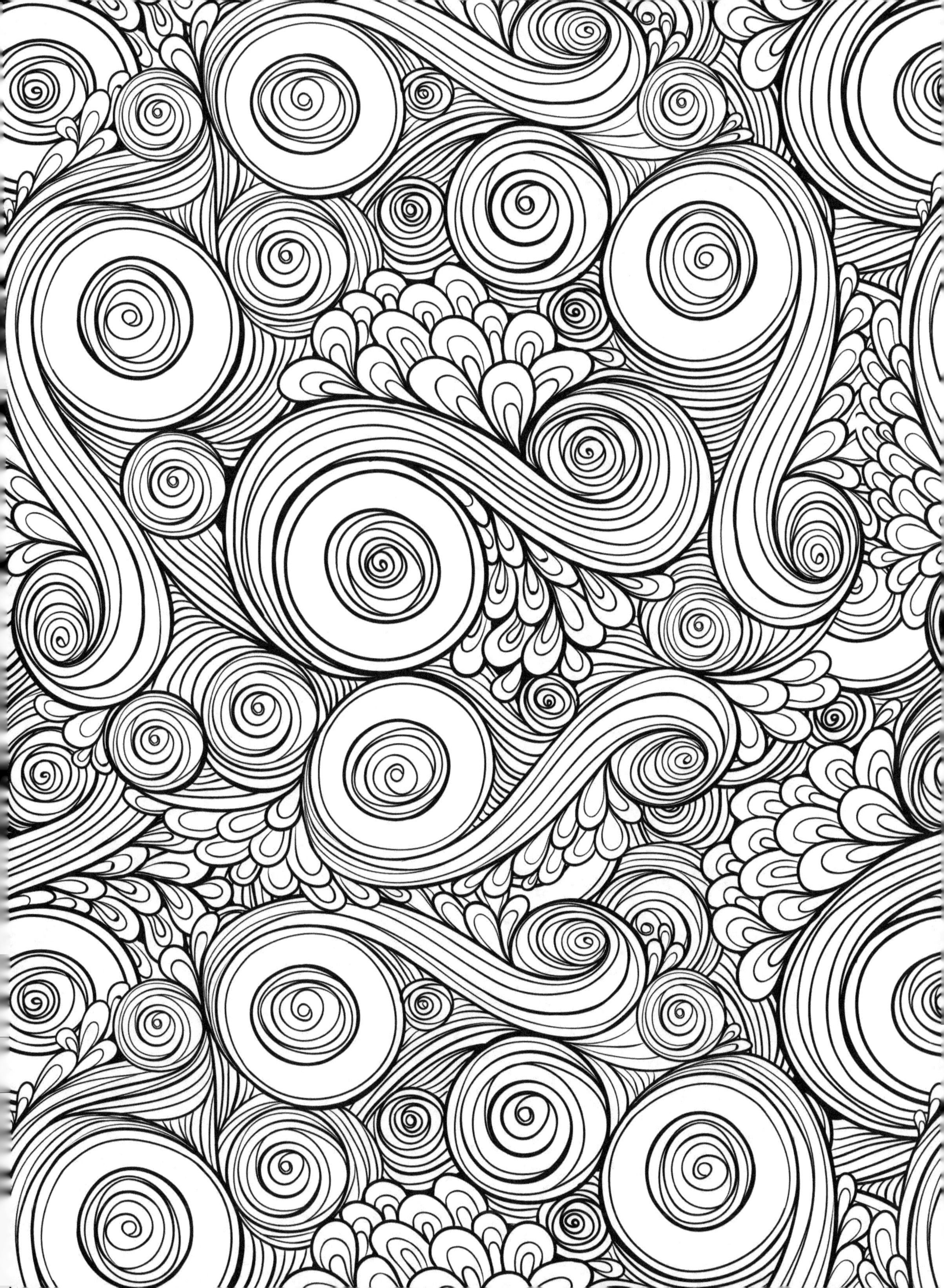

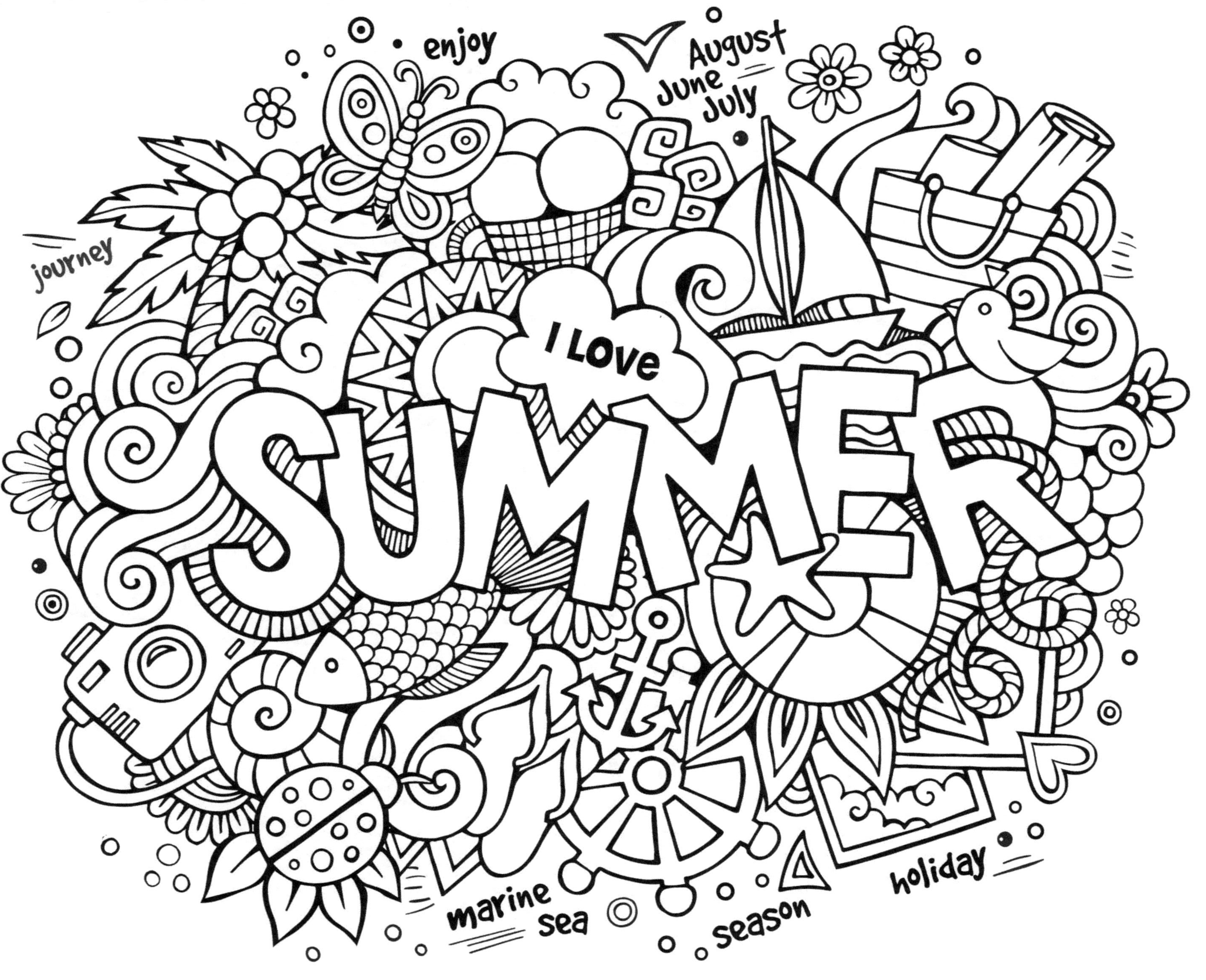
enjoy
August
June
July
journey
I LOVE
SUMMER
marine
sea
season
holiday

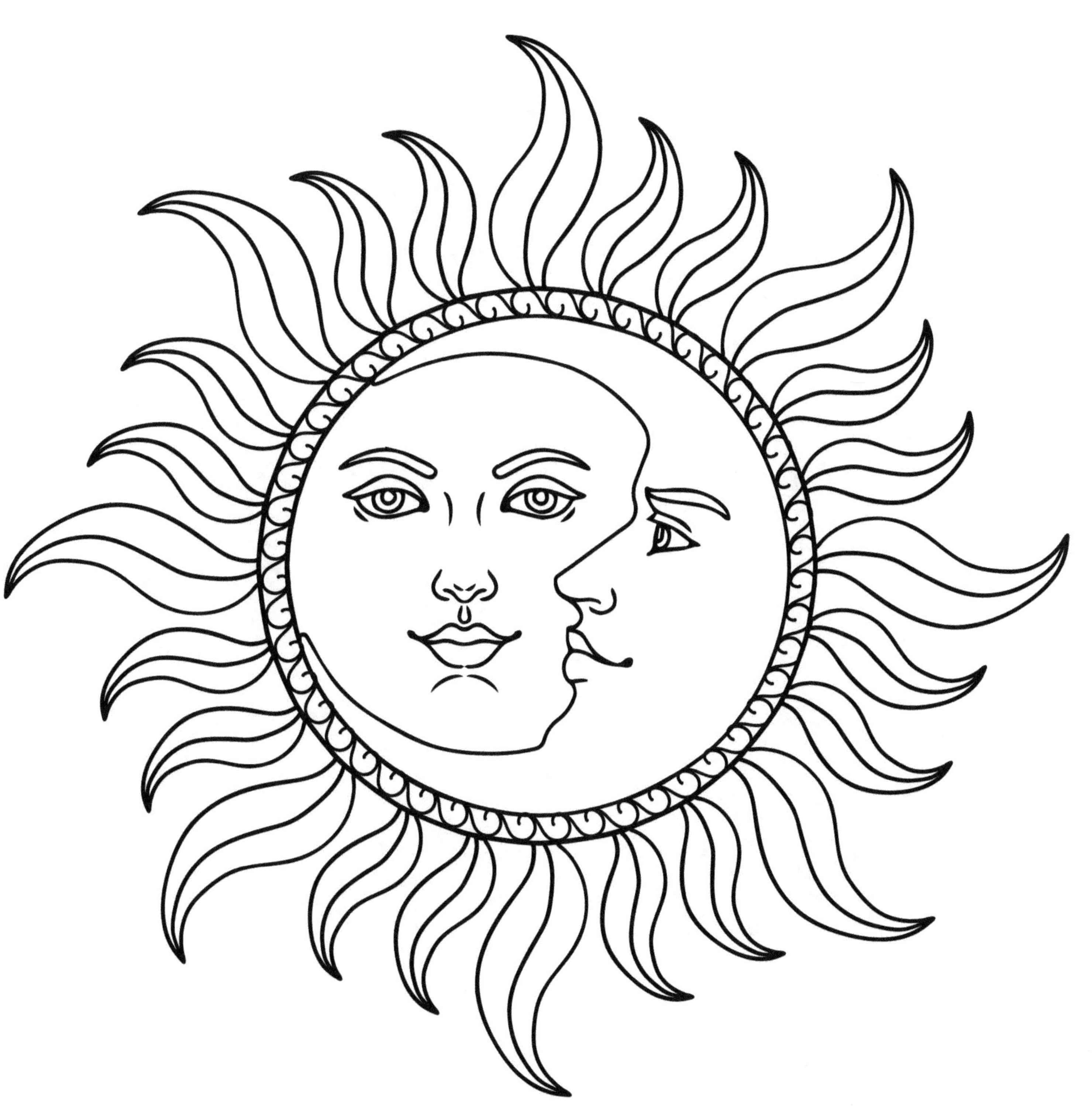

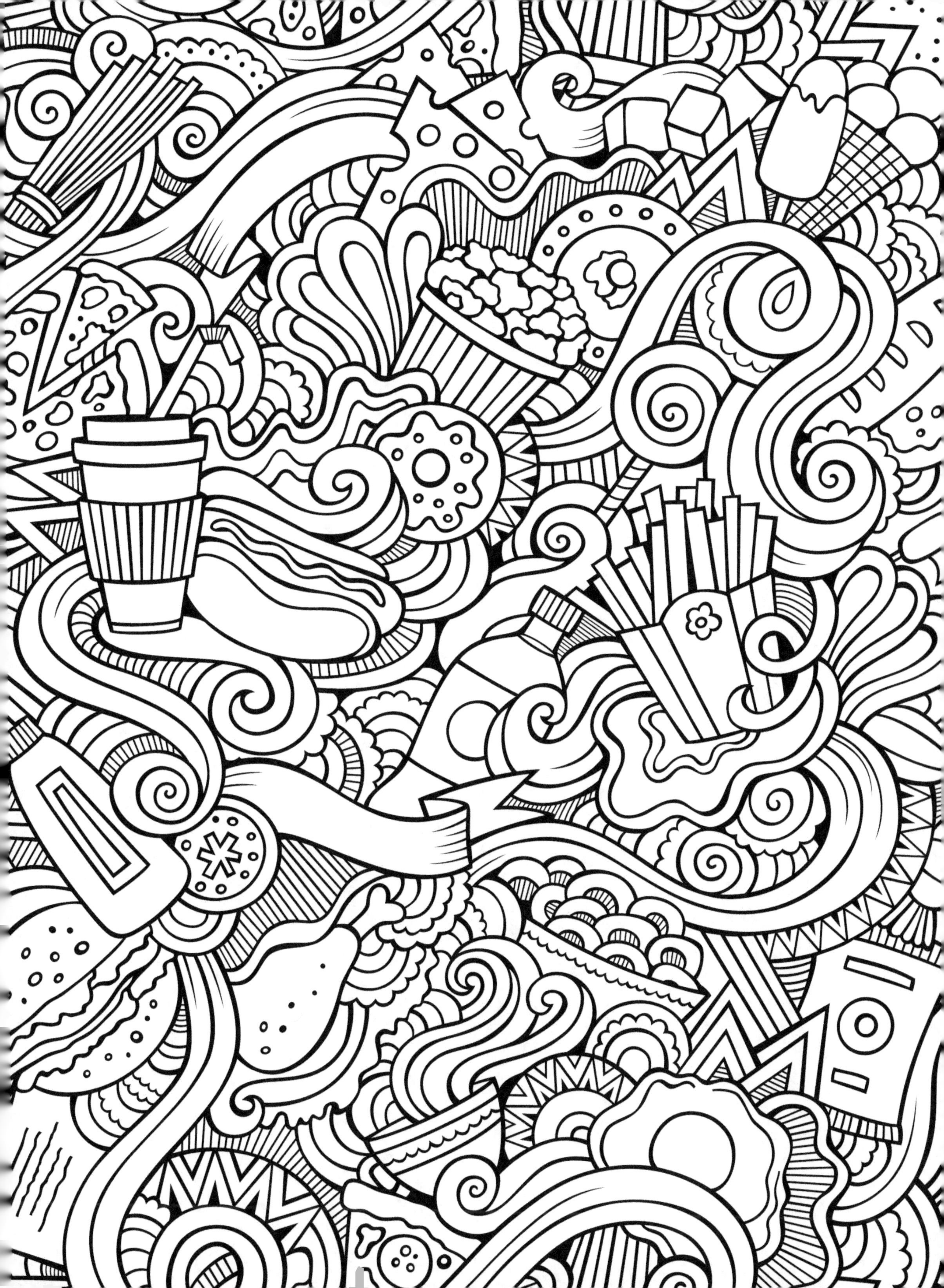

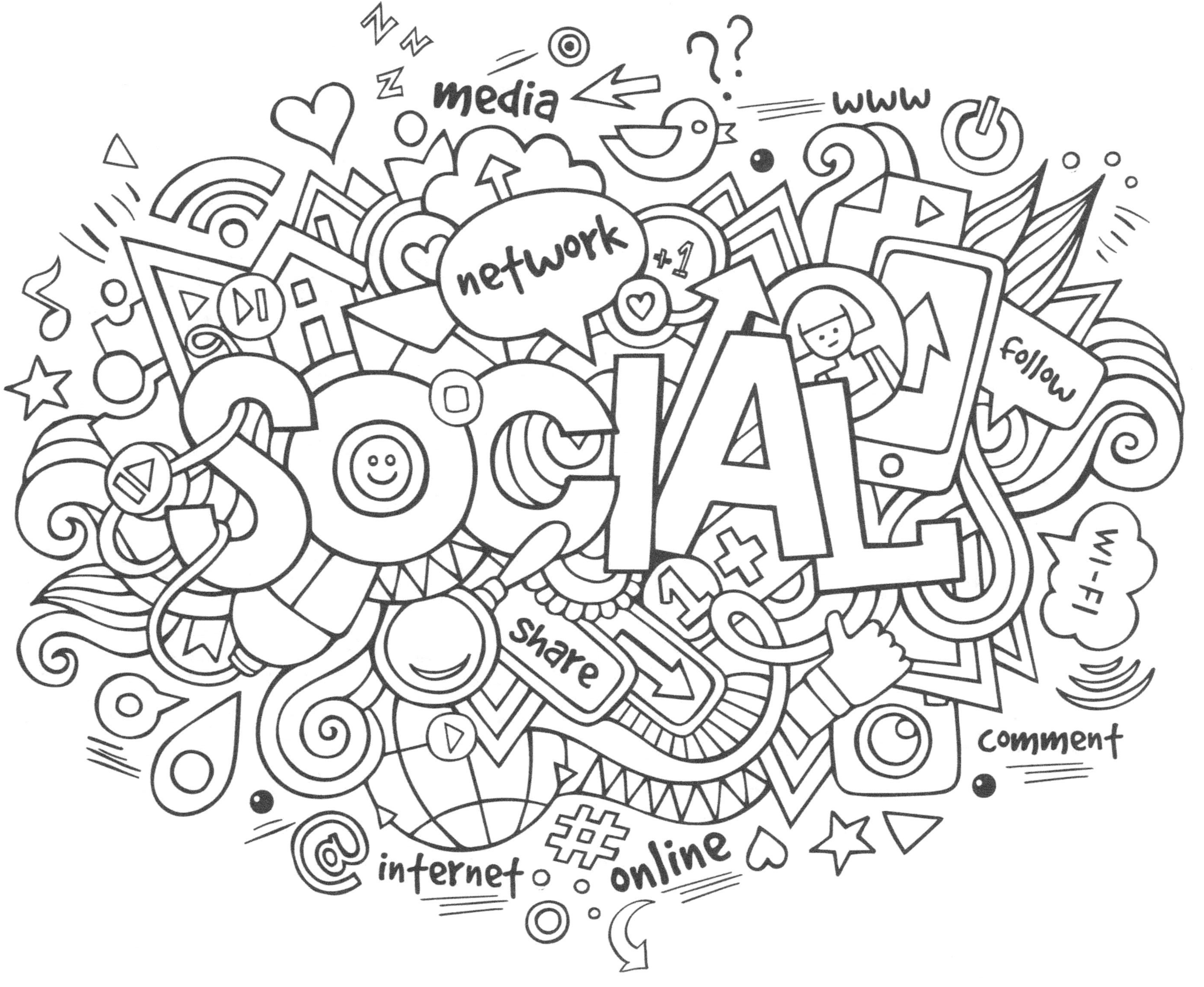
media
www
network
+1
SOCIAL
follow
WI-FI
share
comment
internet
online

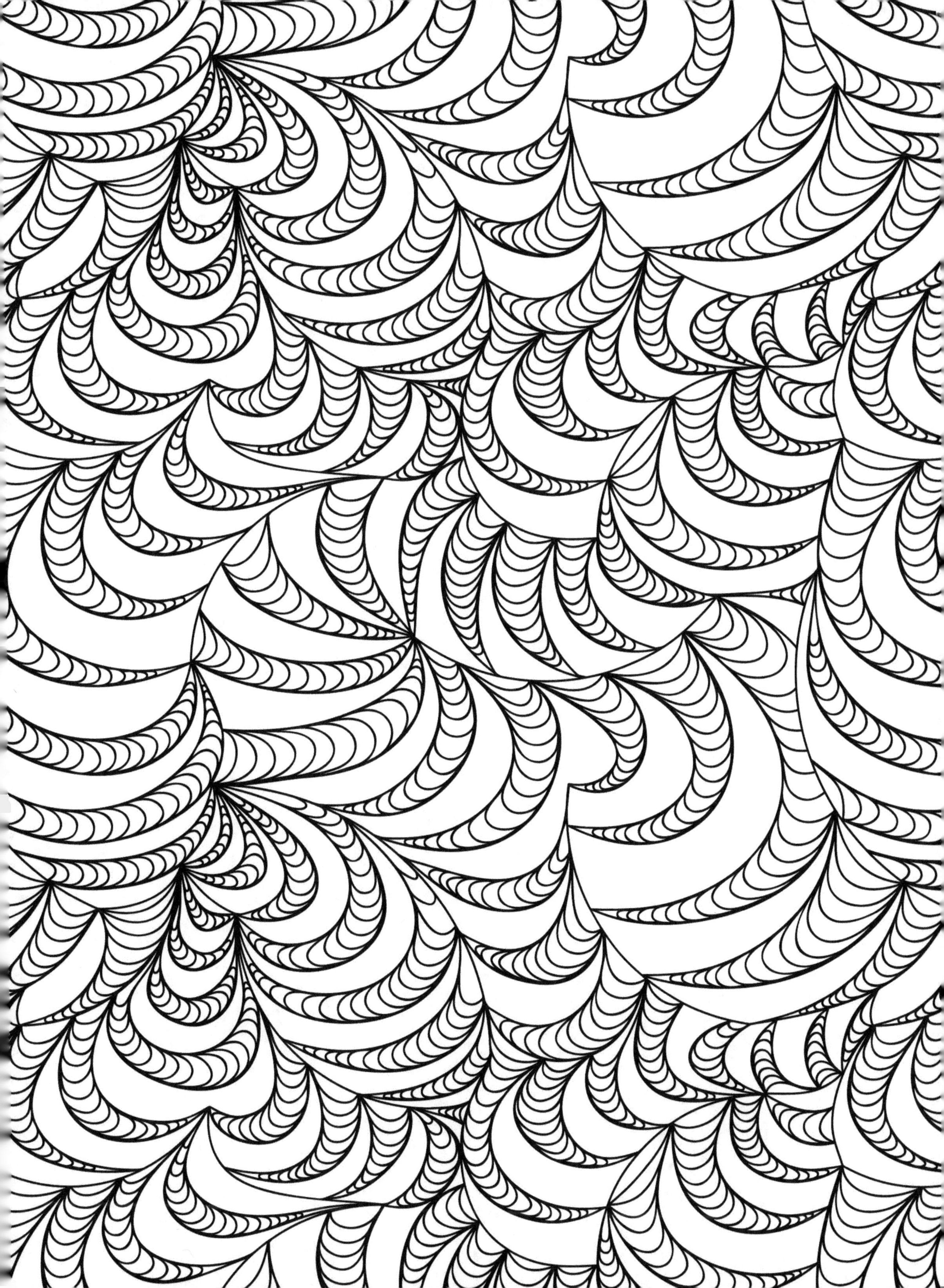

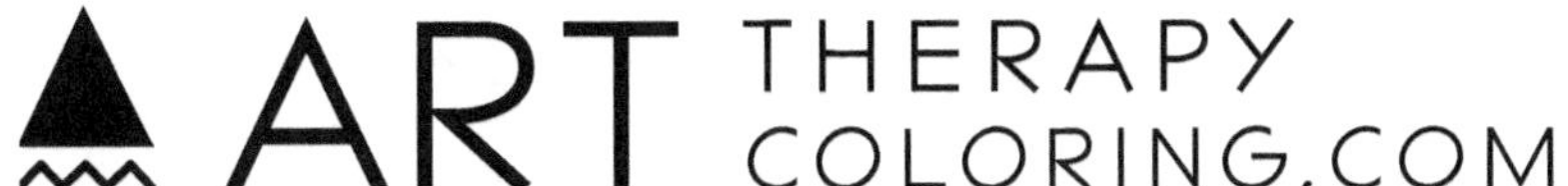

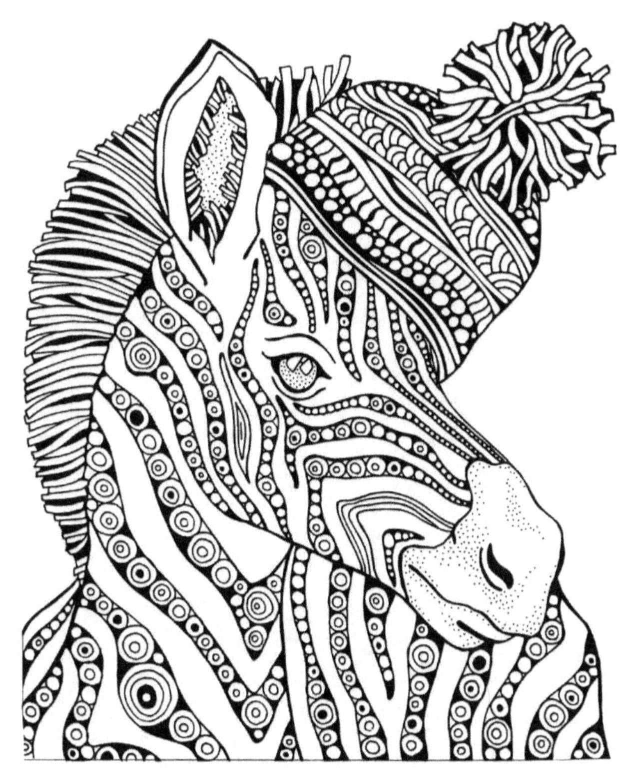

Did You Enjoy Our Coloring Book?

We Want To Hear About It!

Help spread the word about our coloring books! The best way to spread the word is through reviews. We know how busy you are, especially with all of that coloring, but we would appreciate it!

Visit our website at www.arttherapycoloring.com

Over 200 Art Therapy Coloring Books

See our collection of over 200 Art Therapy Coloring Books for Adults, Men, Women, Seniors, Teens, Kids, Boys, and Girls.

Coloring Books For Teens

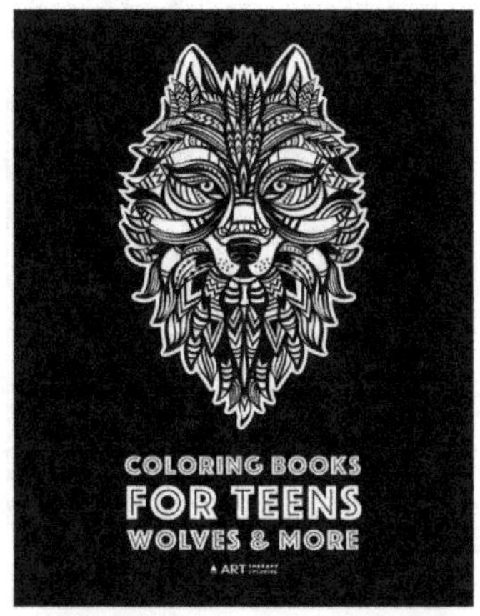

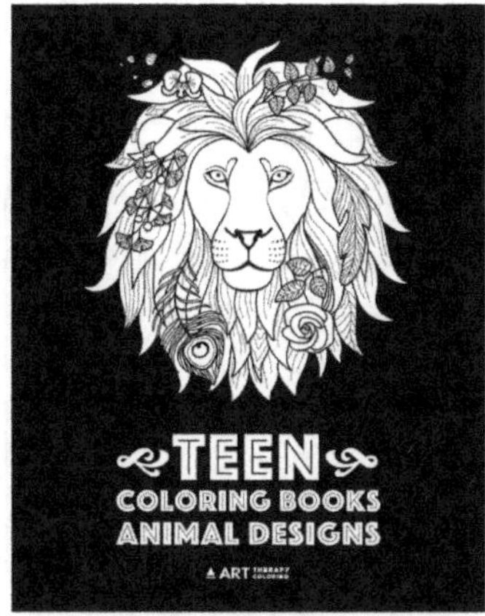

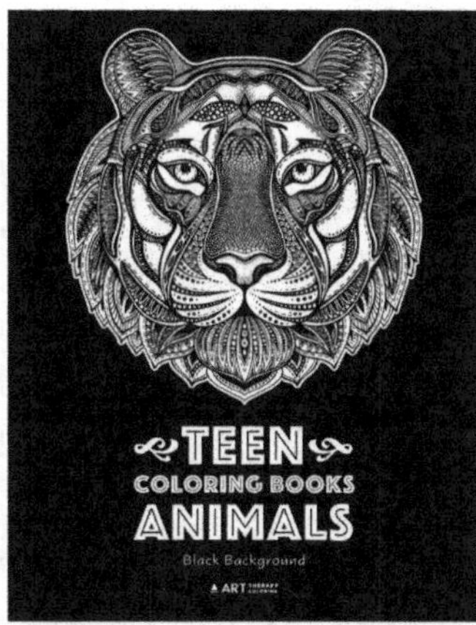

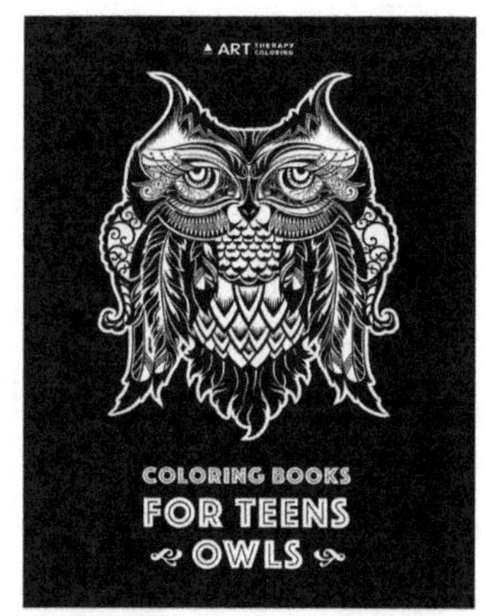

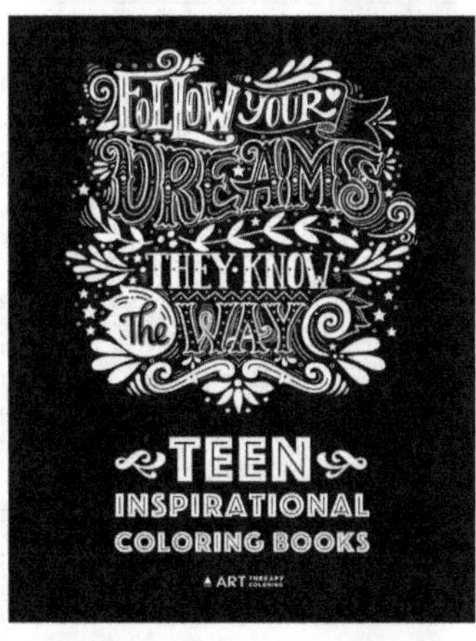

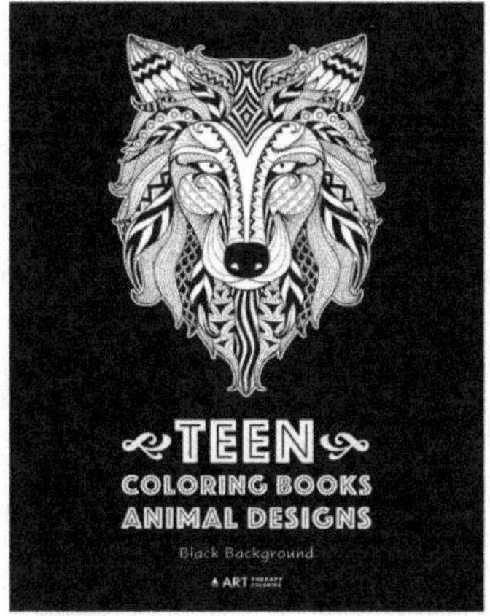

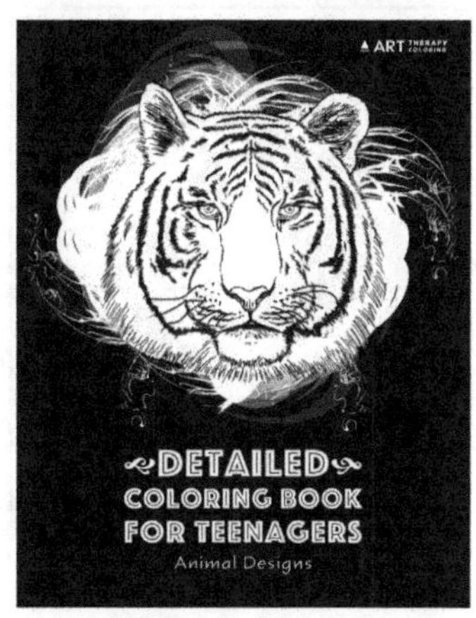

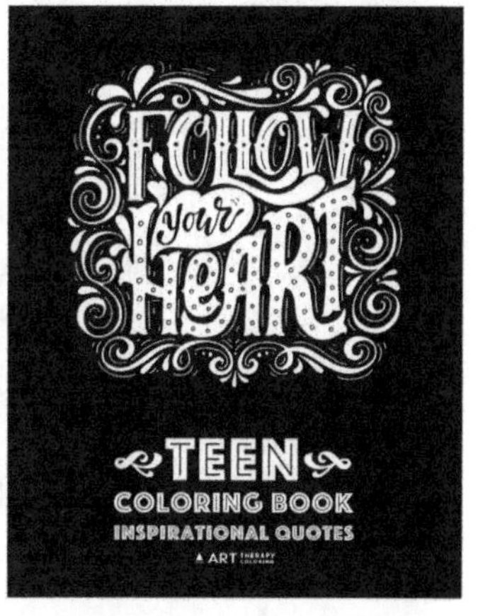

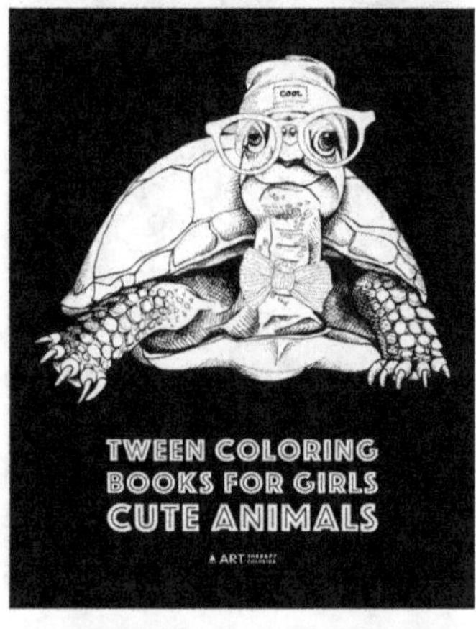

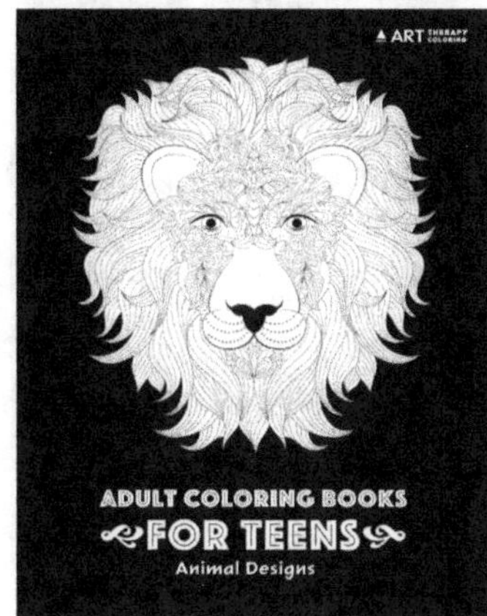

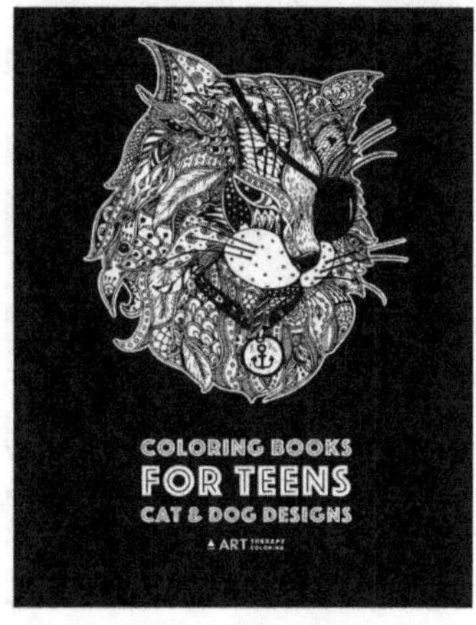

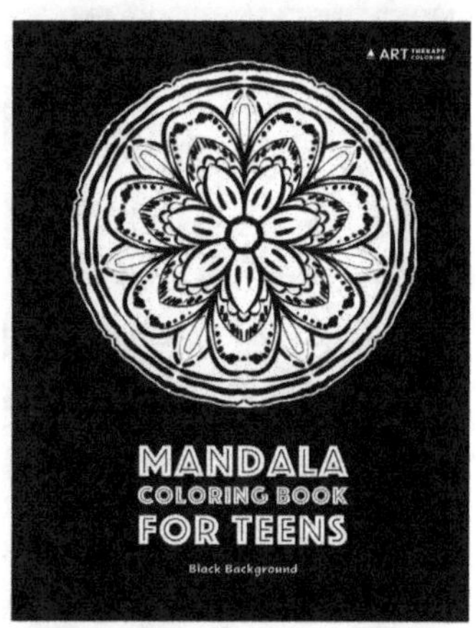

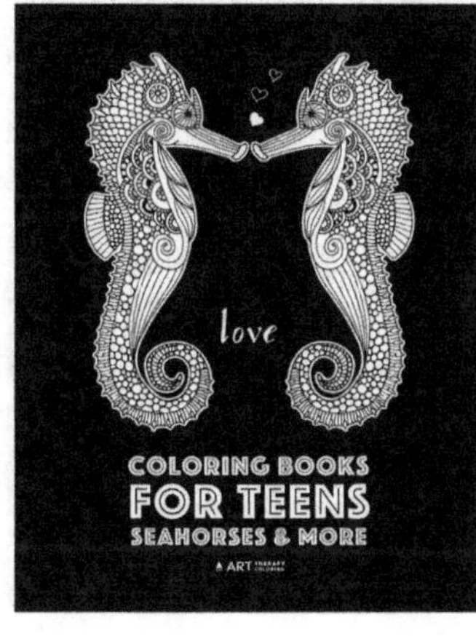

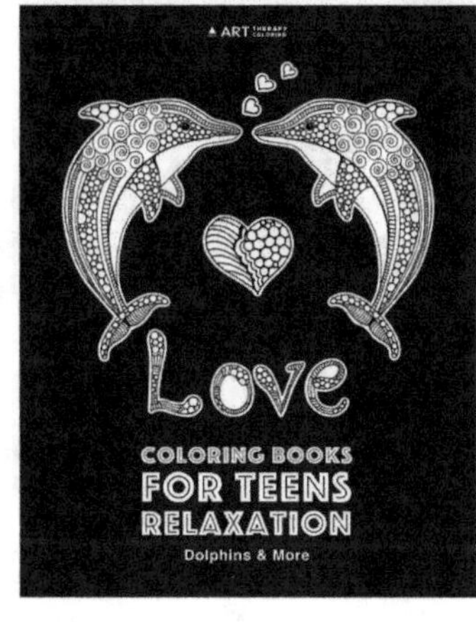

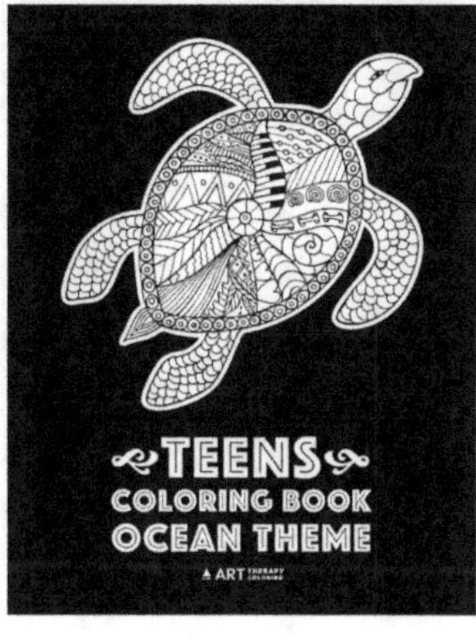

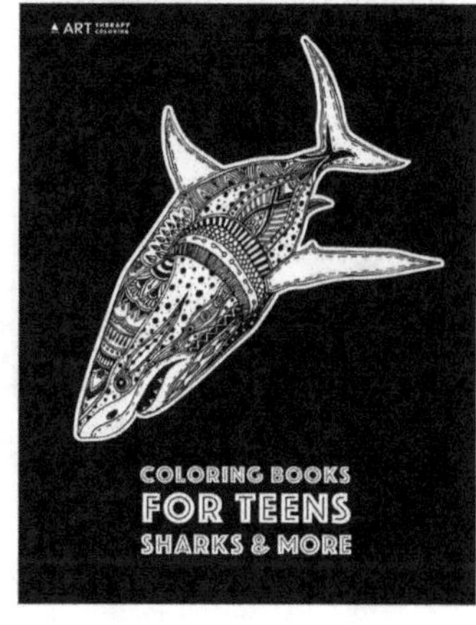

Coloring Books For Teens

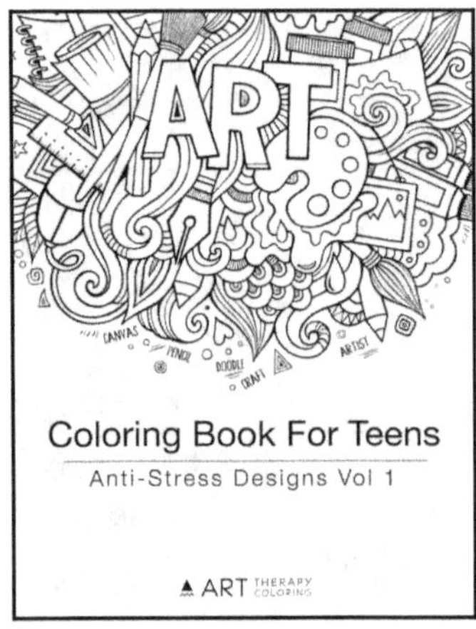

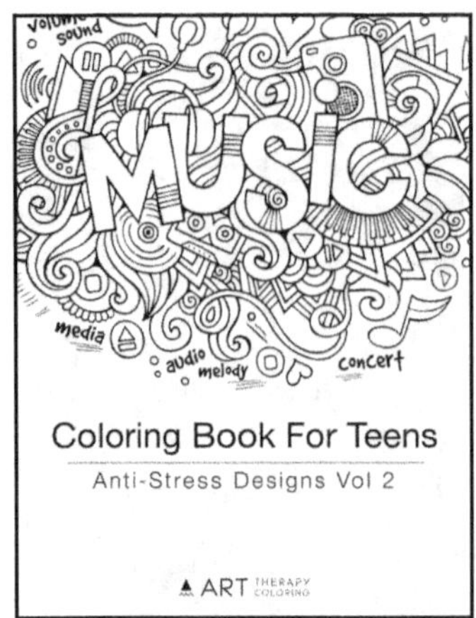

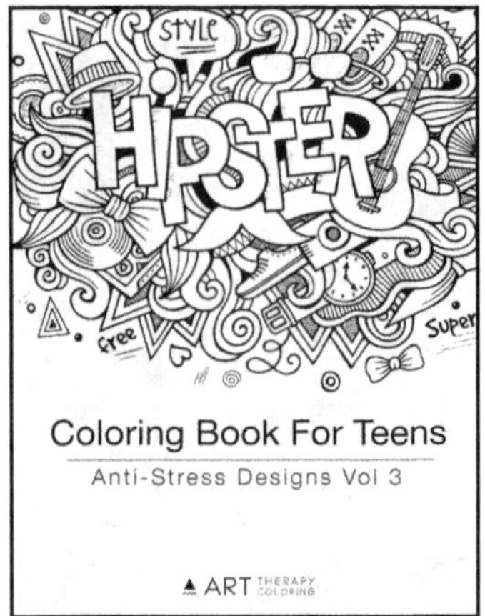

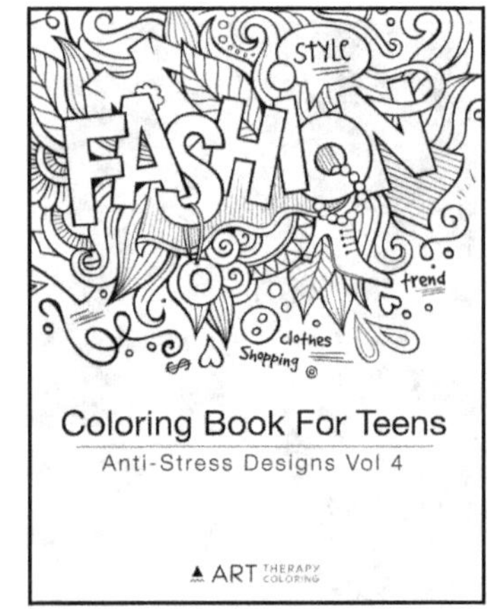

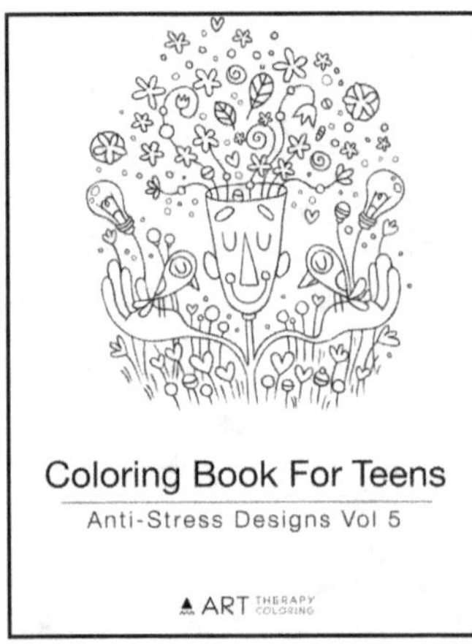

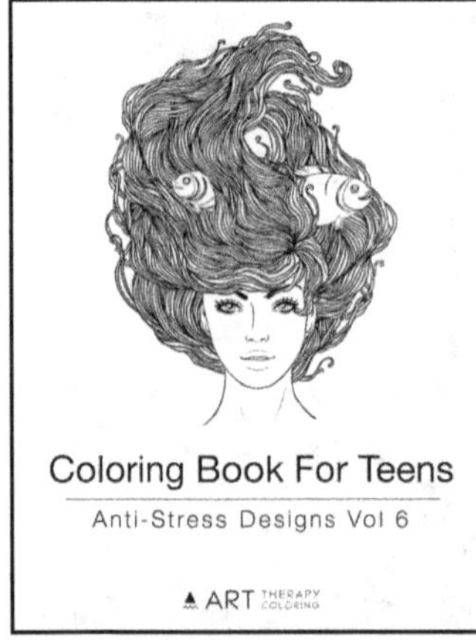

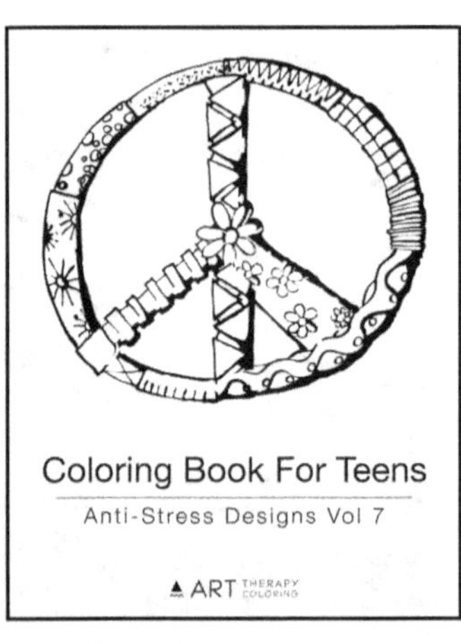

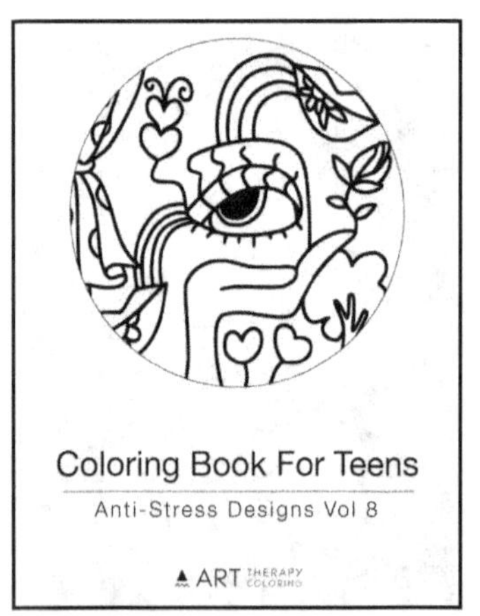

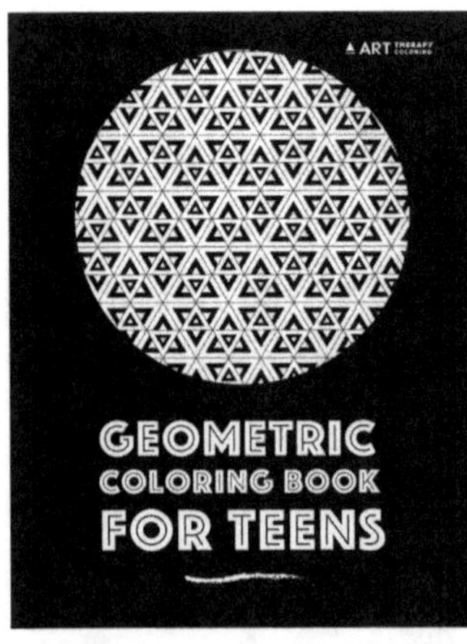

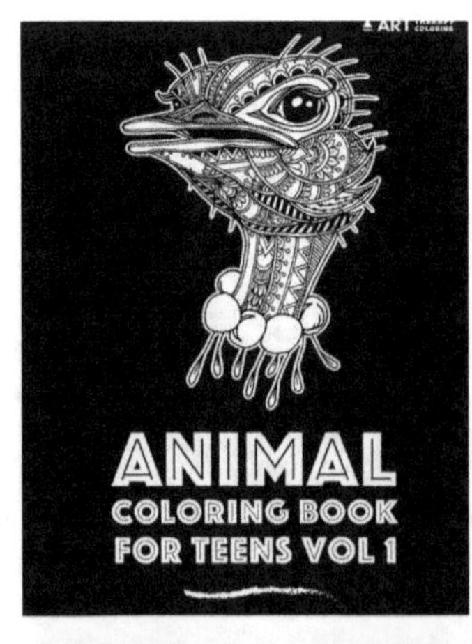

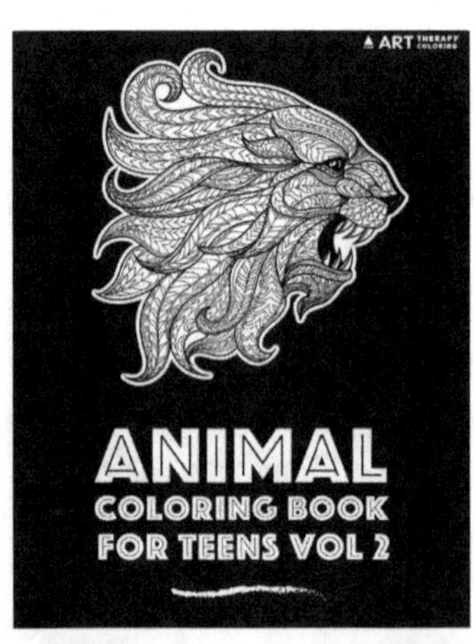

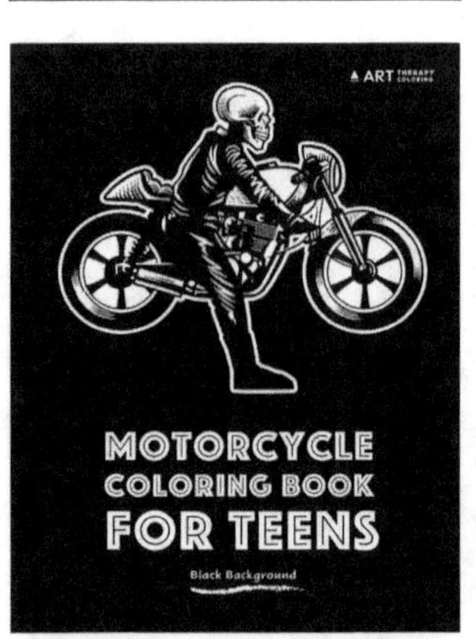

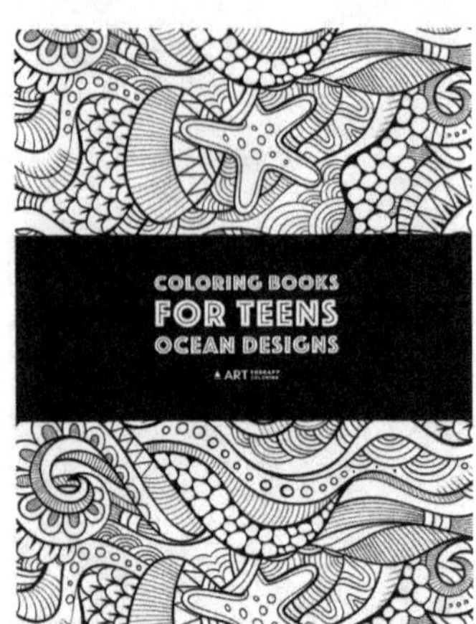

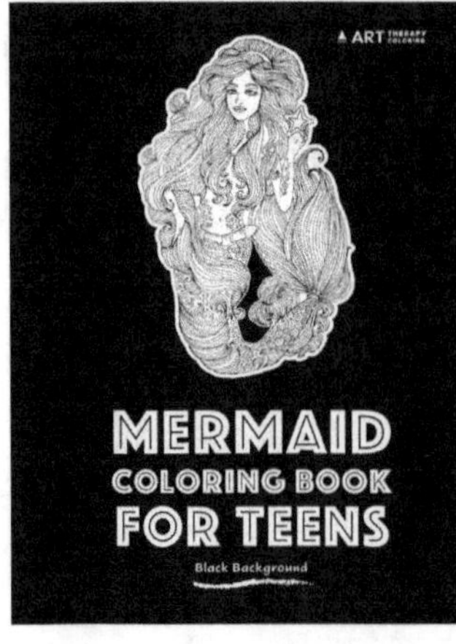

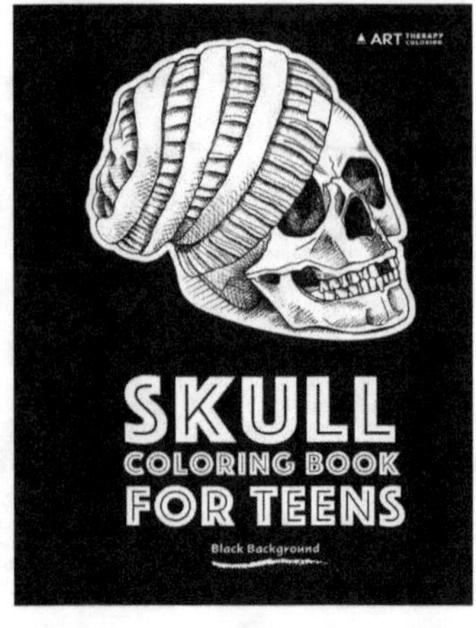

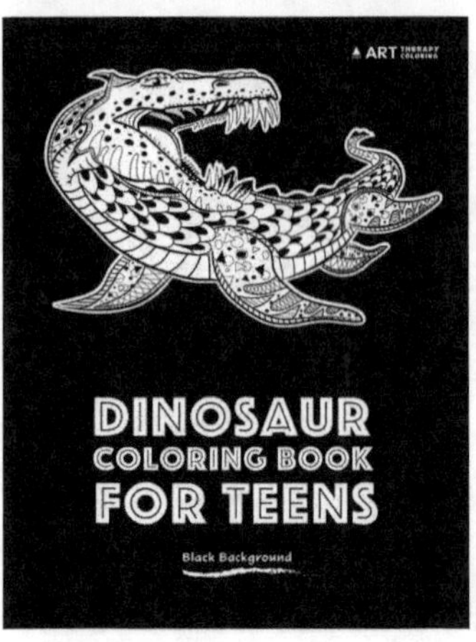

Coloring Books For Girls

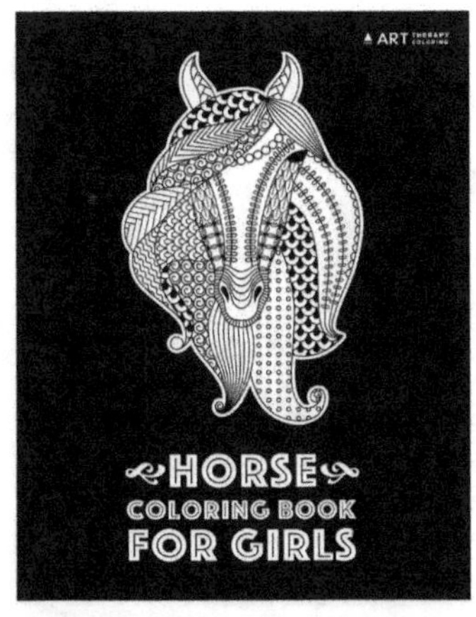

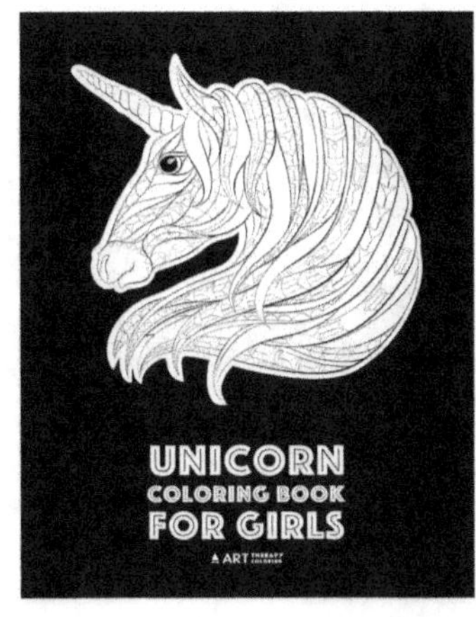

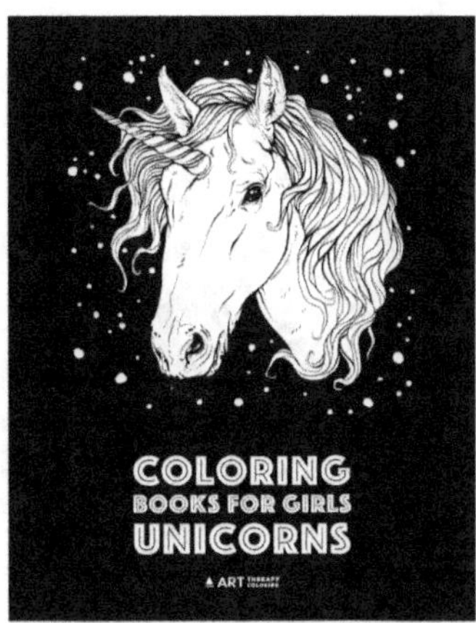

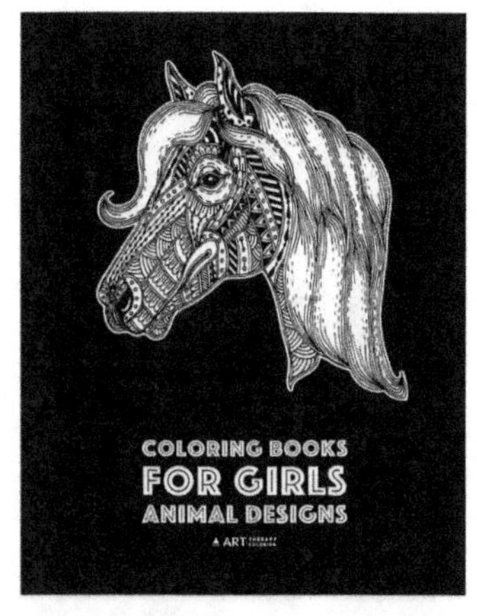

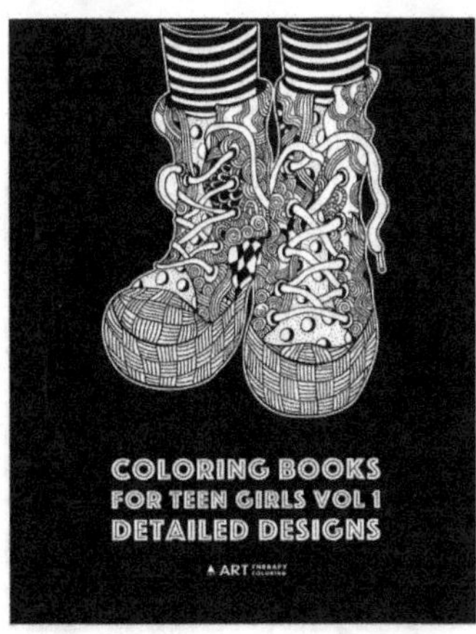

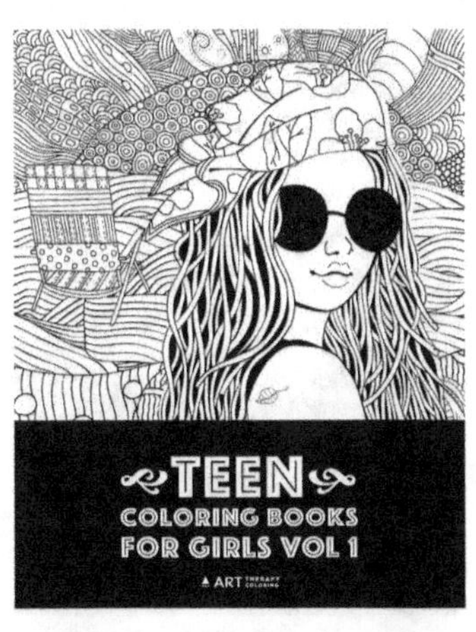

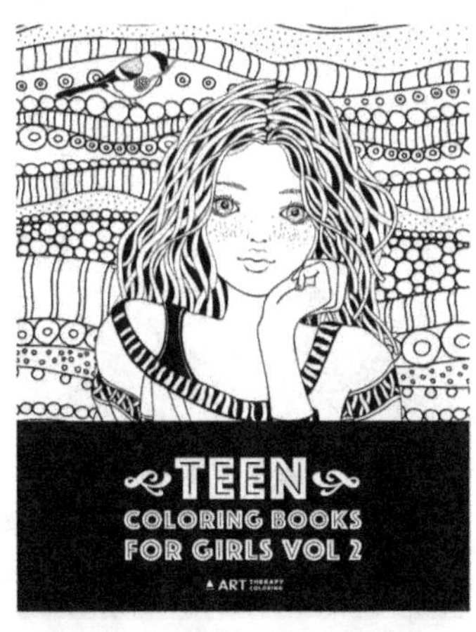

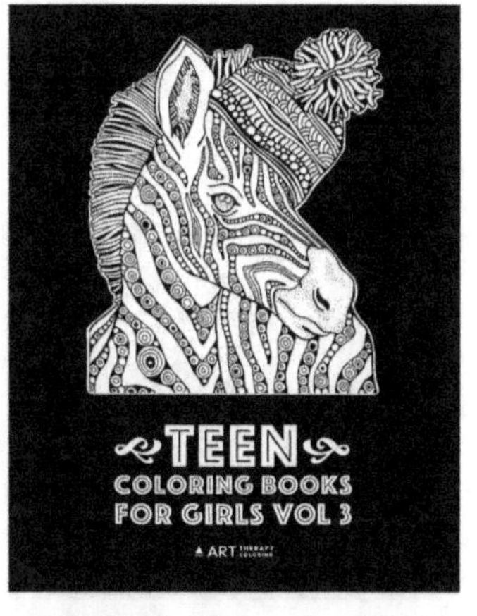

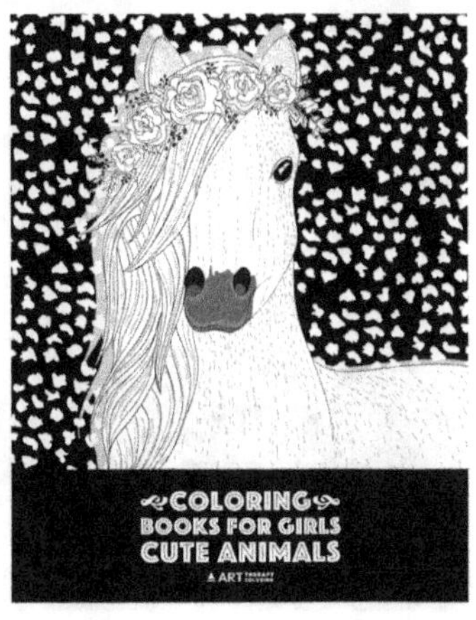

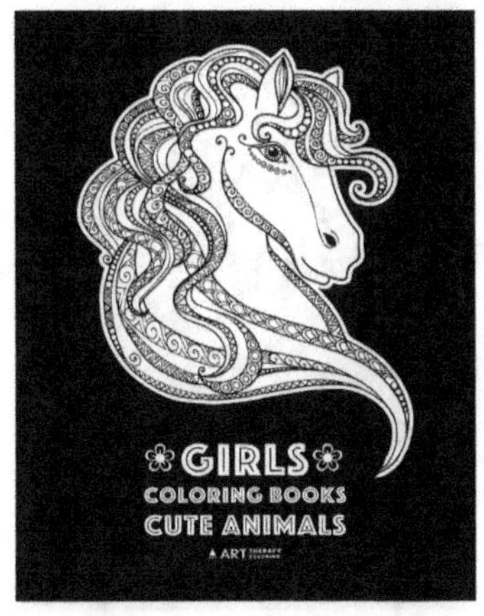

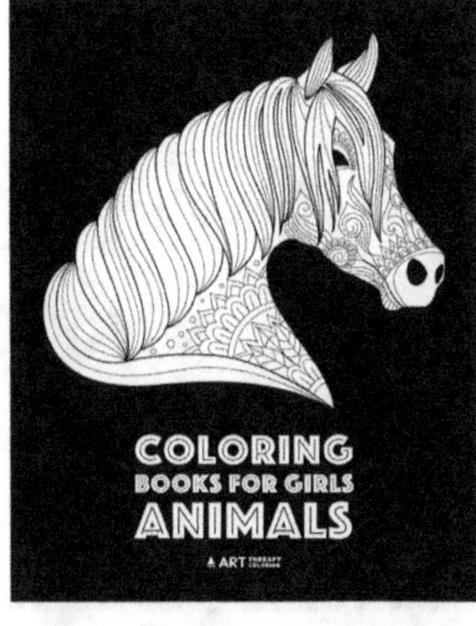

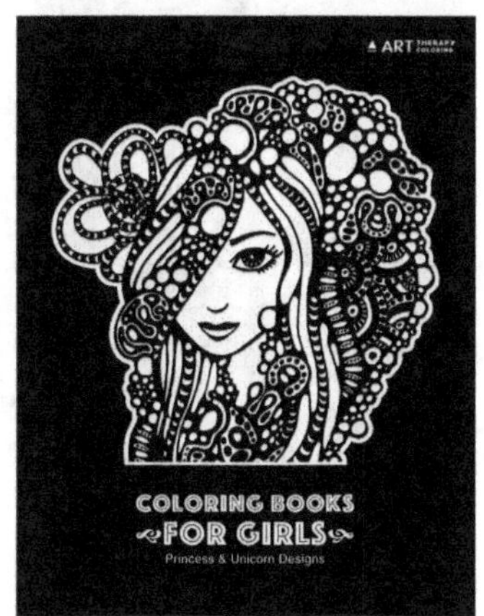

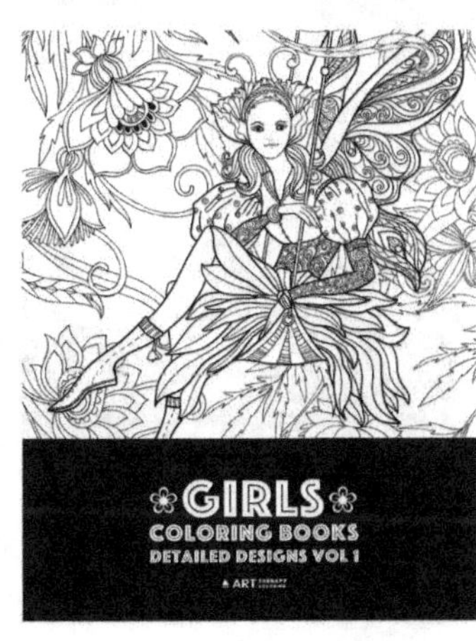

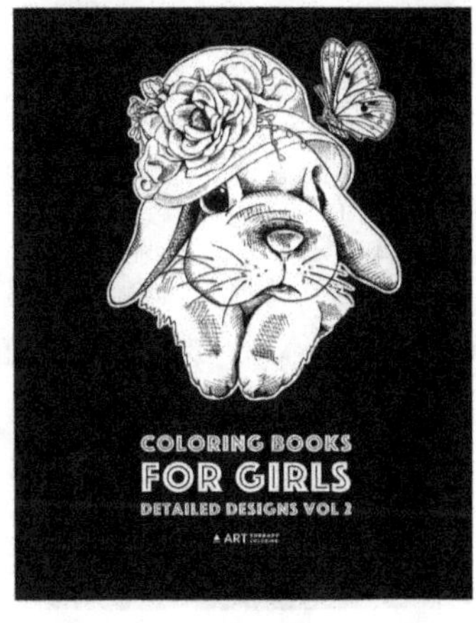

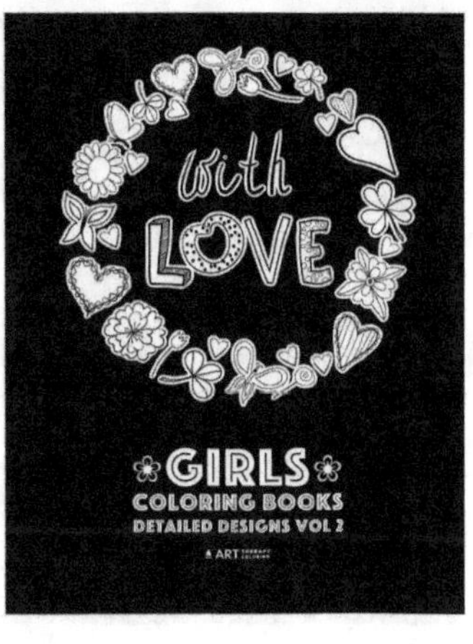

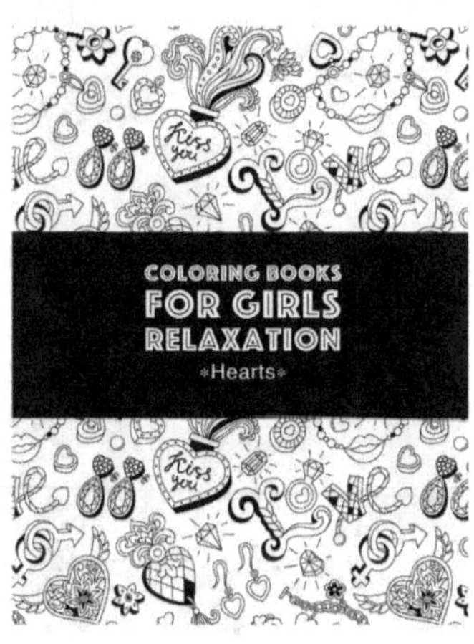

Coloring Books For Boys

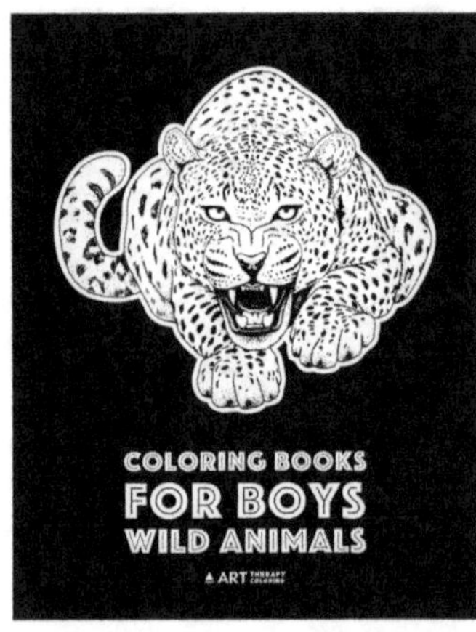
COLORING BOOKS
FOR BOYS
WILD ANIMALS
ART

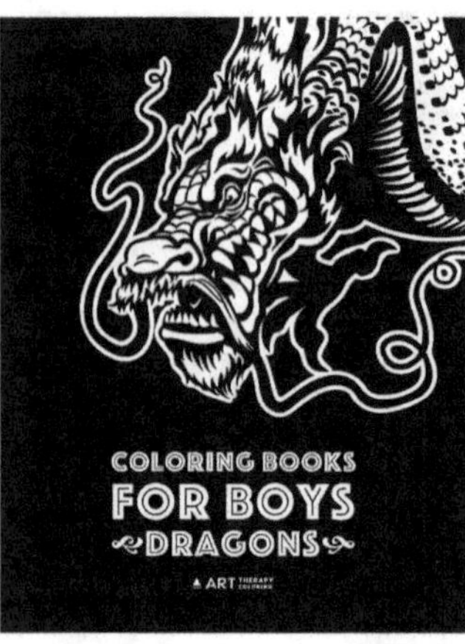
COLORING BOOKS
FOR BOYS
DRAGONS
ART

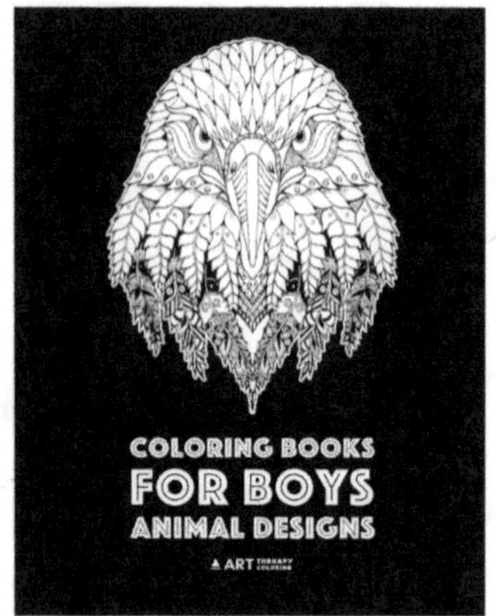
COLORING BOOKS
FOR BOYS
ANIMAL DESIGNS
ART

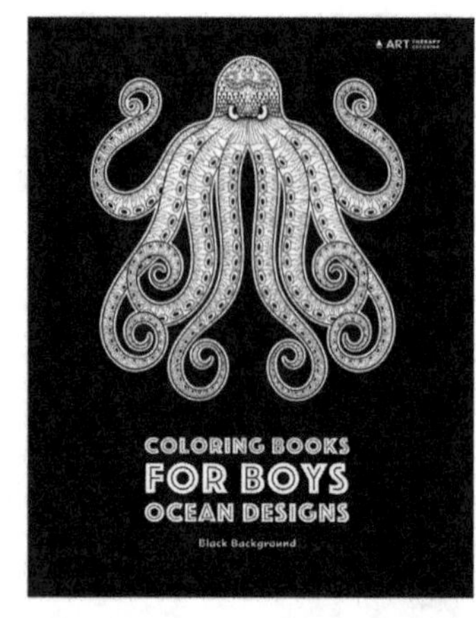
ART
COLORING BOOKS
FOR BOYS
OCEAN DESIGNS
Black Background

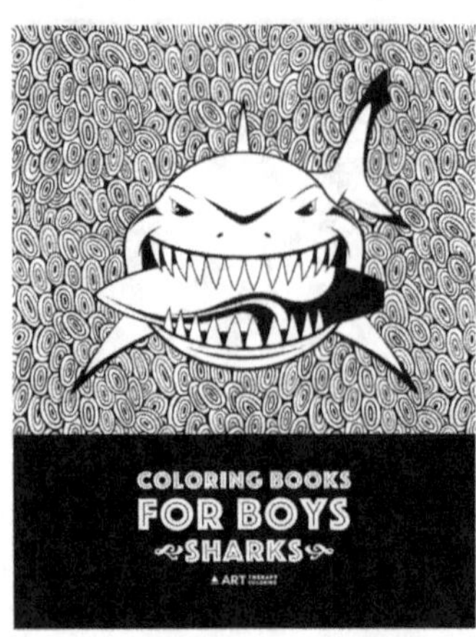
COLORING BOOKS
FOR BOYS
SHARKS
ART

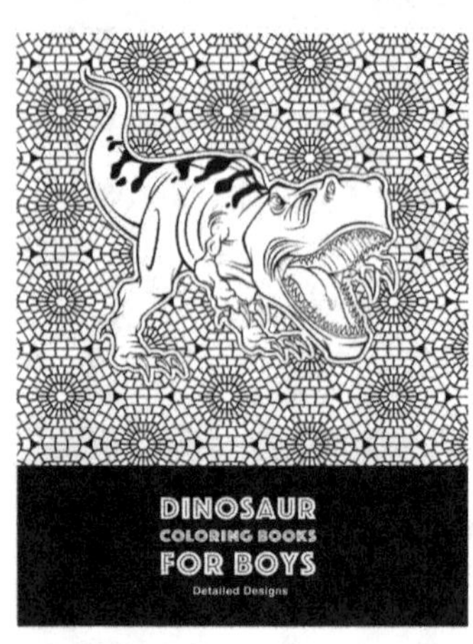
DINOSAUR
COLORING BOOKS
FOR BOYS
Detailed Designs

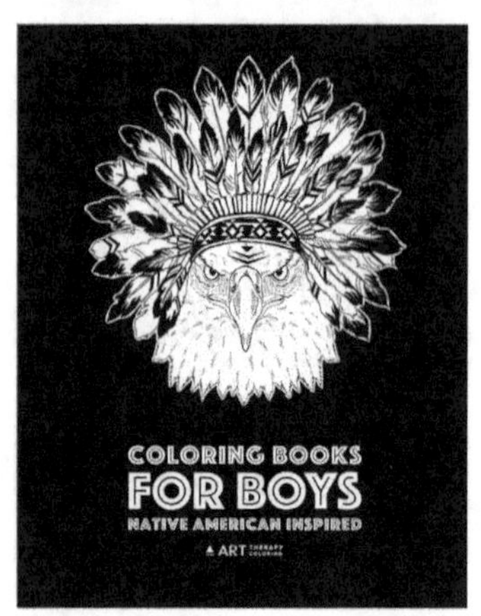
COLORING BOOKS
FOR BOYS
NATIVE AMERICAN INSPIRED
ART

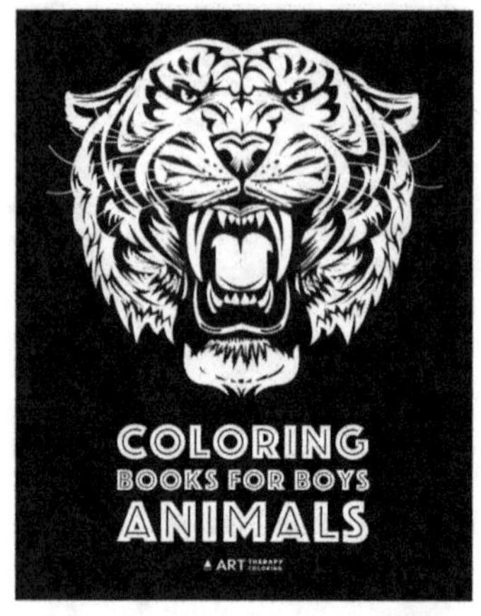
COLORING
BOOKS FOR BOYS
ANIMALS
ART

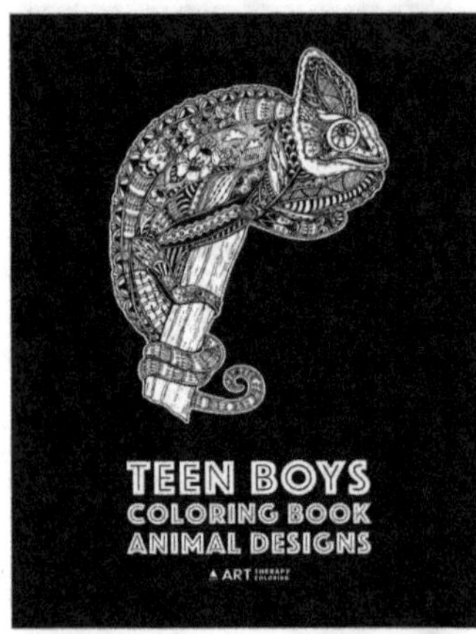
TEEN BOYS
COLORING BOOK
ANIMAL DESIGNS
ART

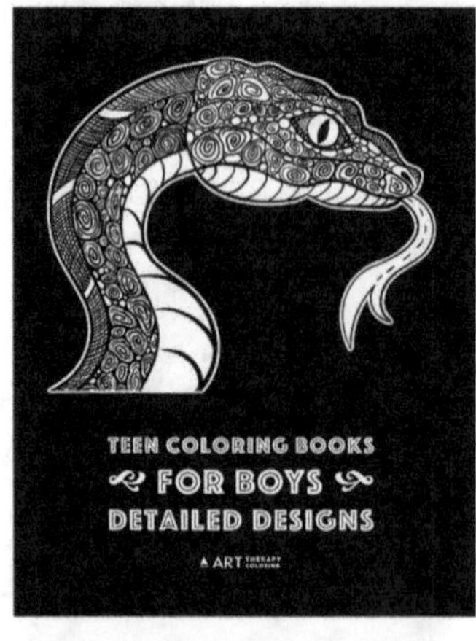
TEEN COLORING BOOKS
FOR BOYS
DETAILED DESIGNS
ART

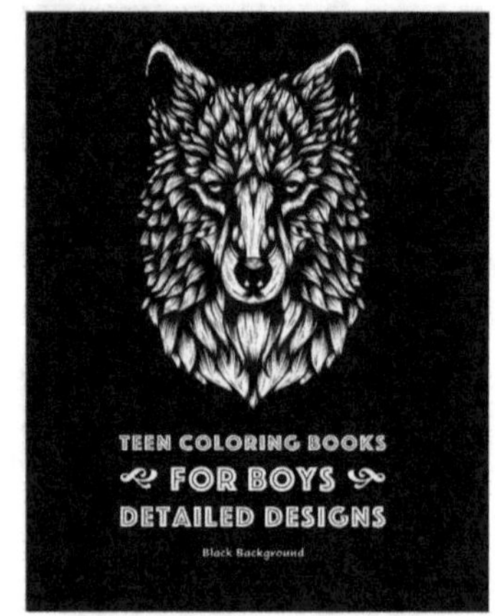
TEEN COLORING BOOKS
FOR BOYS
DETAILED DESIGNS
Black Background

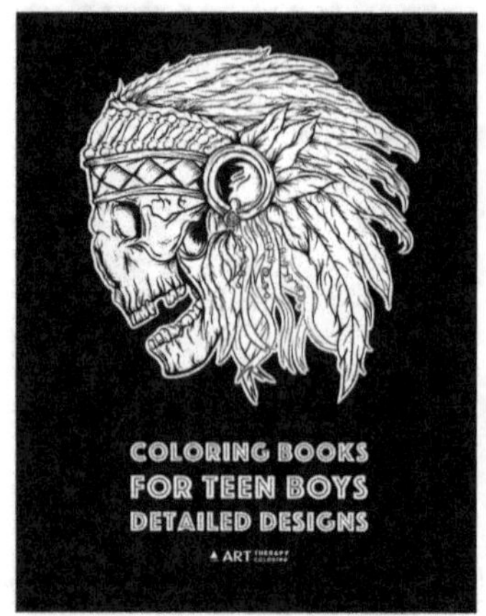
COLORING BOOKS
FOR TEEN BOYS
DETAILED DESIGNS
ART

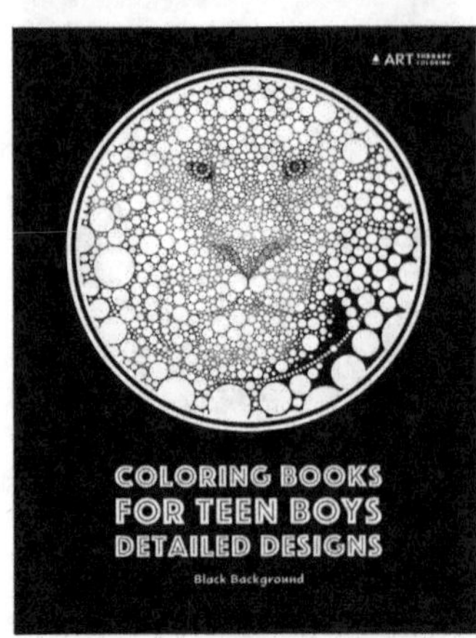
ART
COLORING BOOKS
FOR TEEN BOYS
DETAILED DESIGNS
Black Background

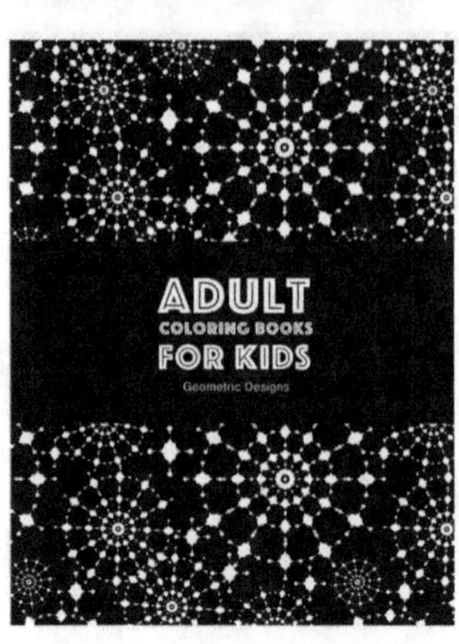
ADULT
COLORING BOOKS
FOR KIDS
Geometric Designs

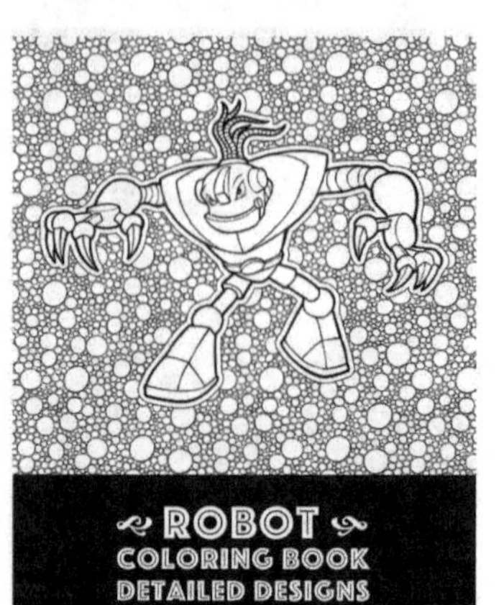
ROBOT
COLORING BOOK
DETAILED DESIGNS

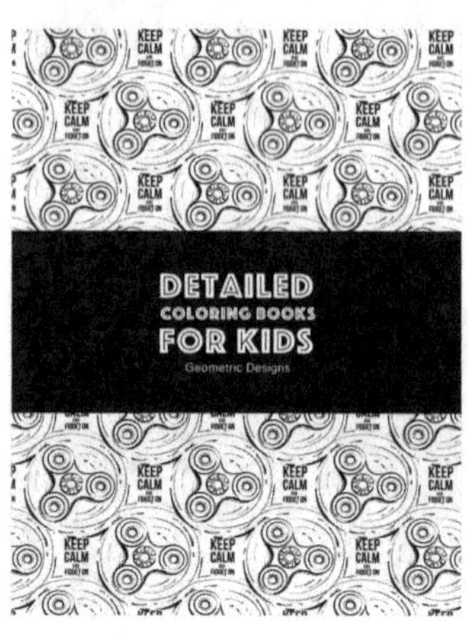
DETAILED
COLORING BOOKS
FOR KIDS
Geometric Designs

Art Therapy Coloring Books

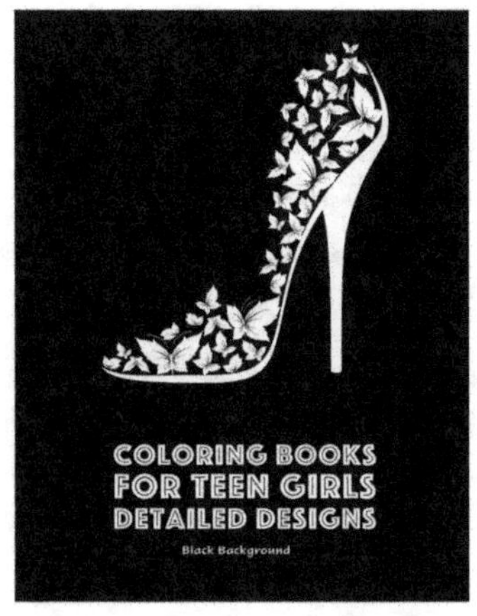

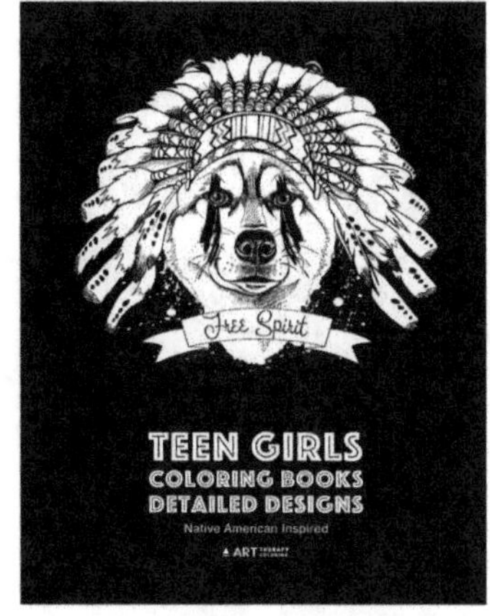

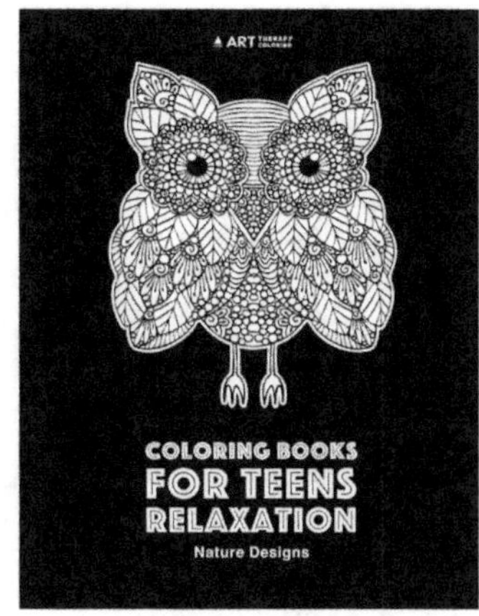

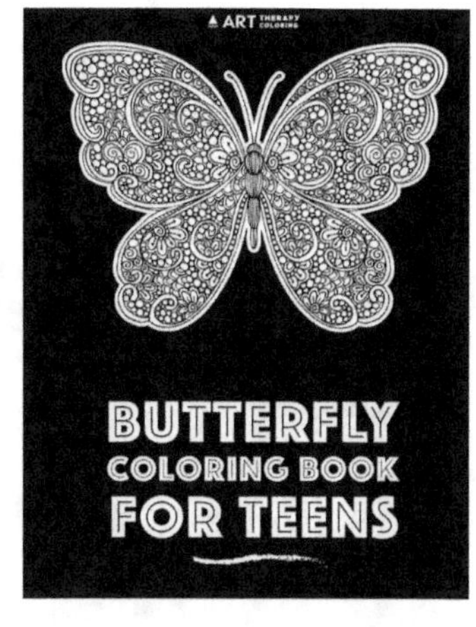

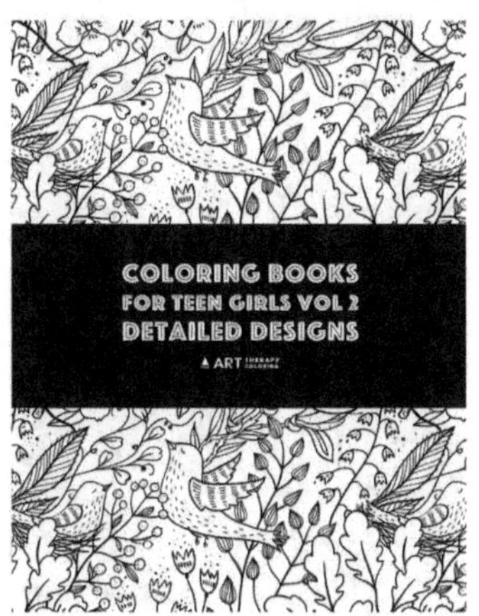

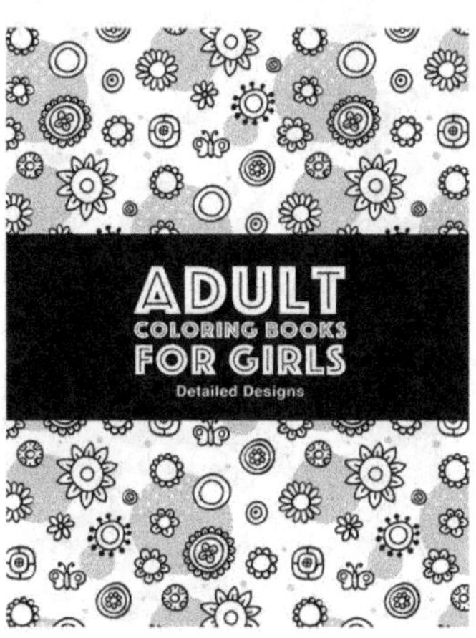

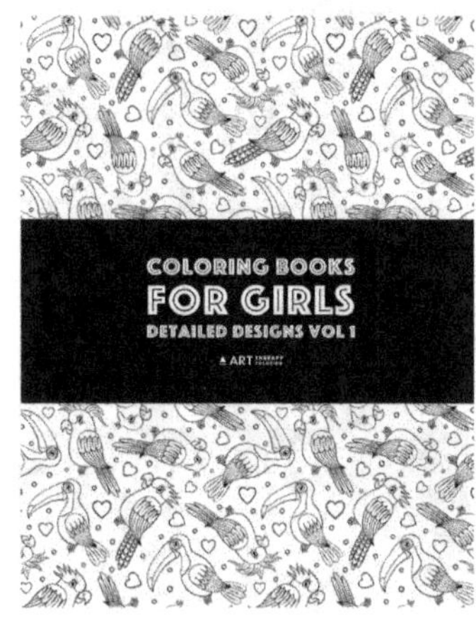

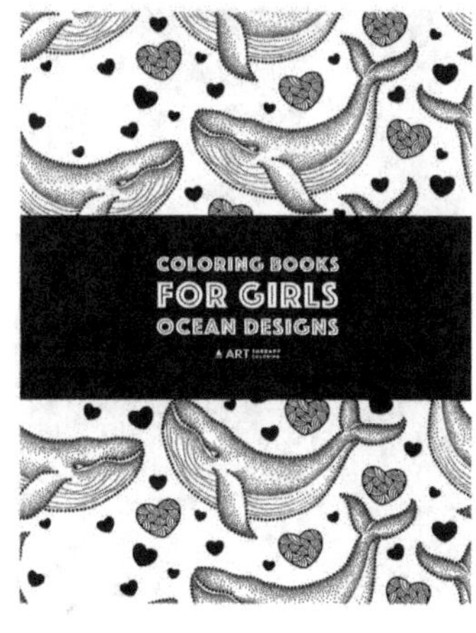

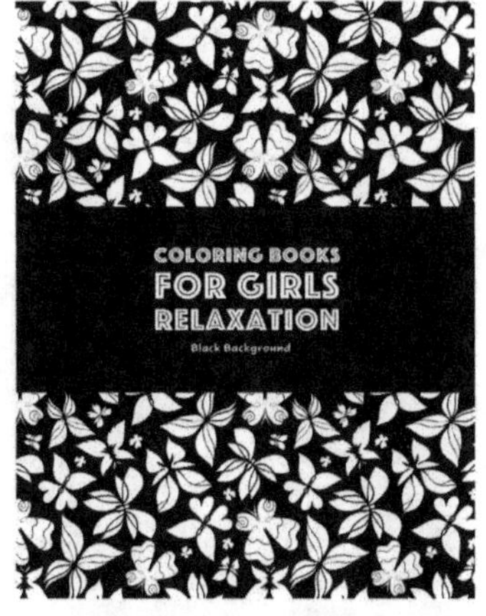

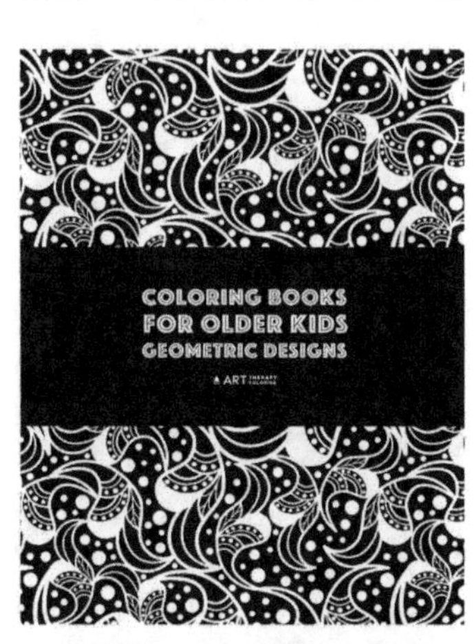

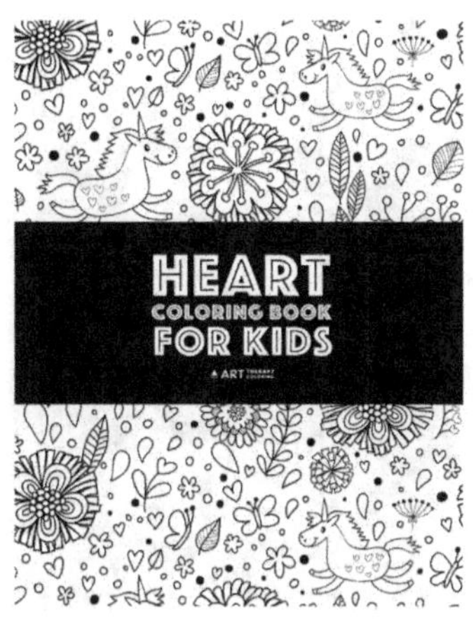

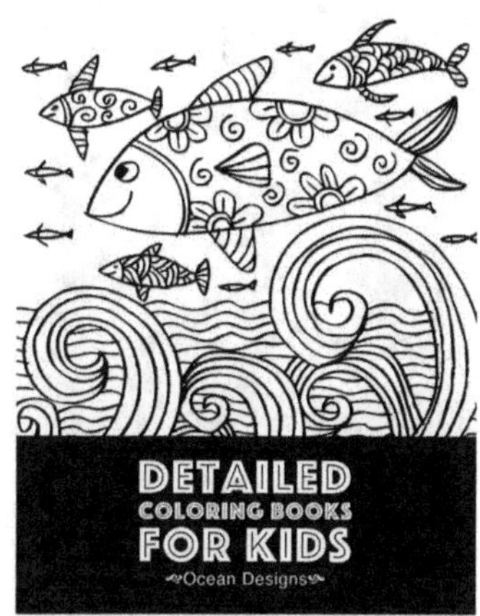

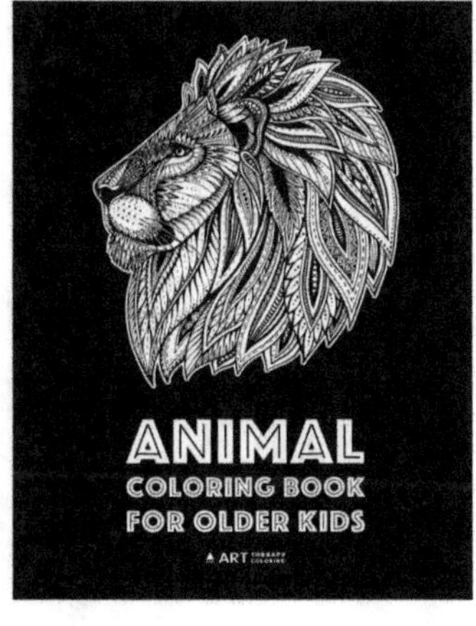

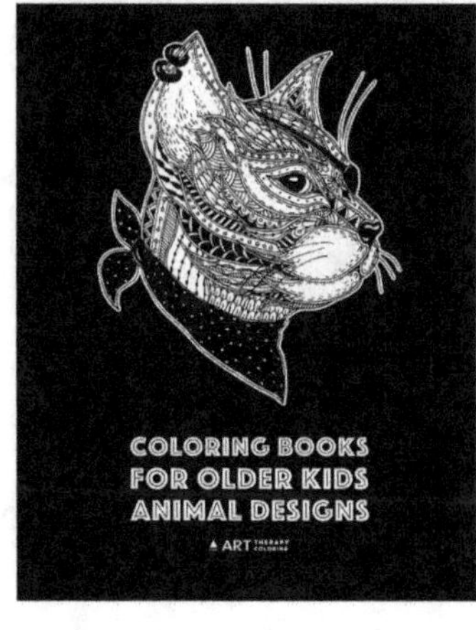

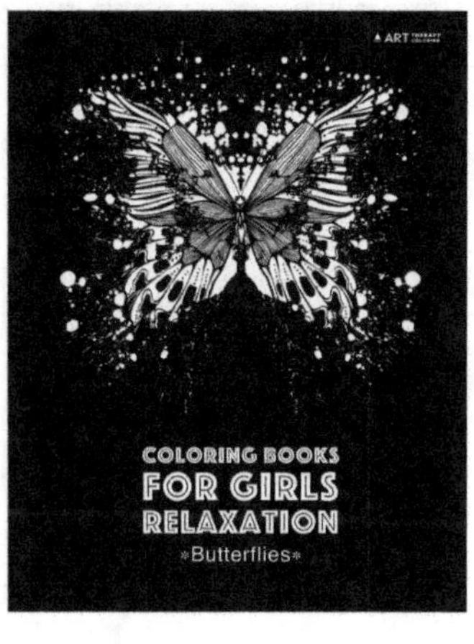

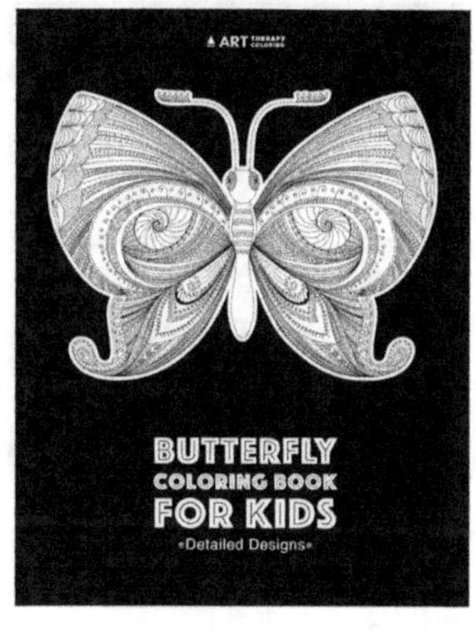

Coloring Books For Kids

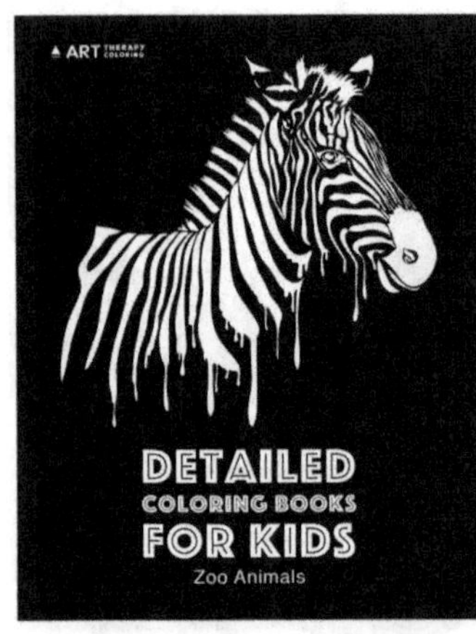

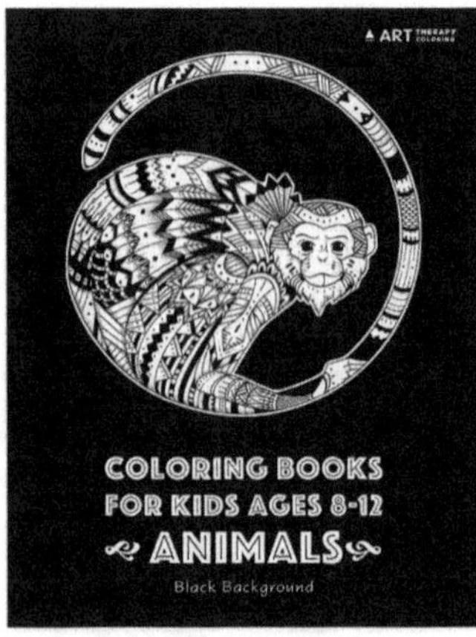

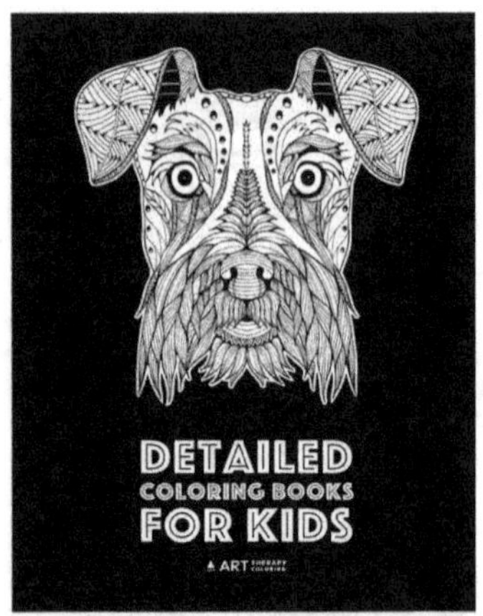

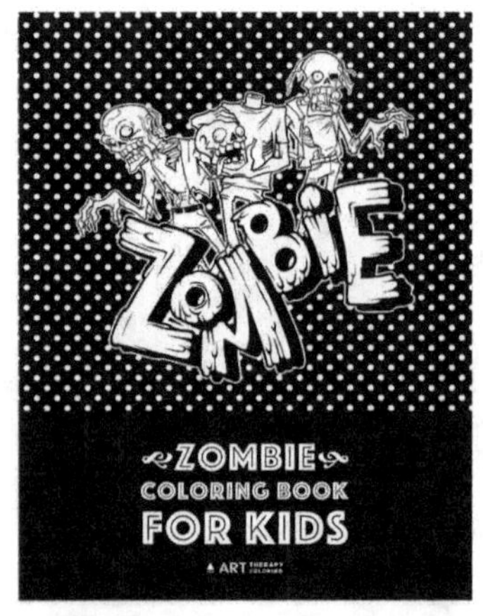

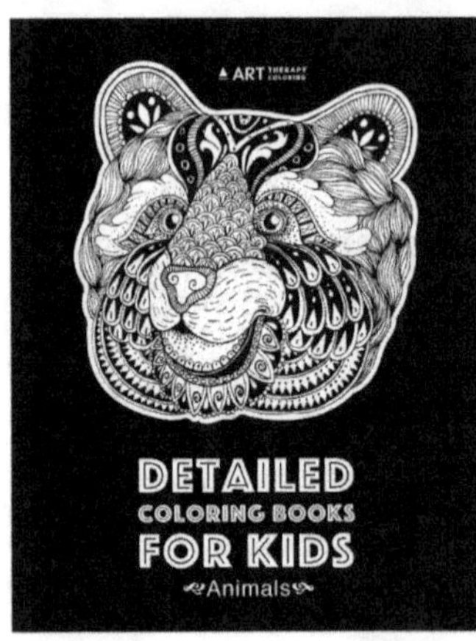

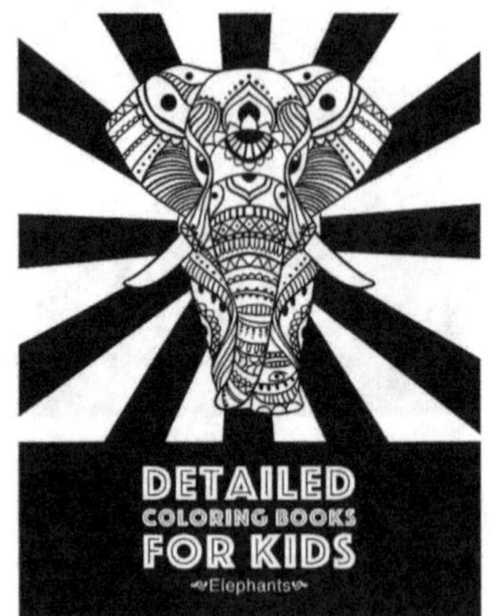

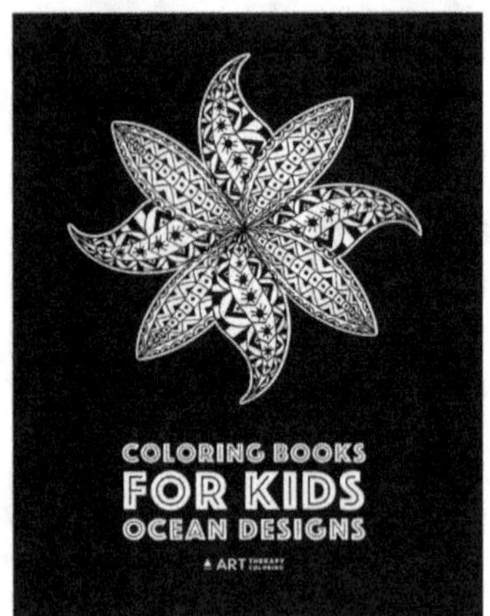

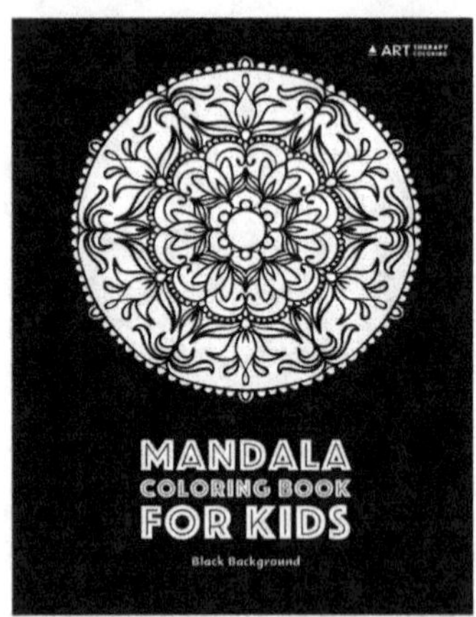

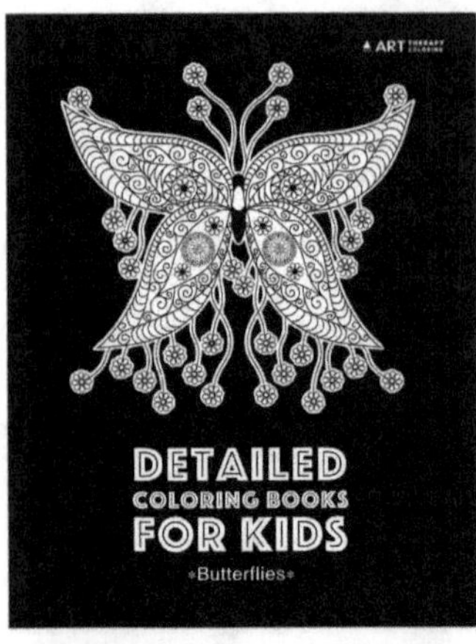

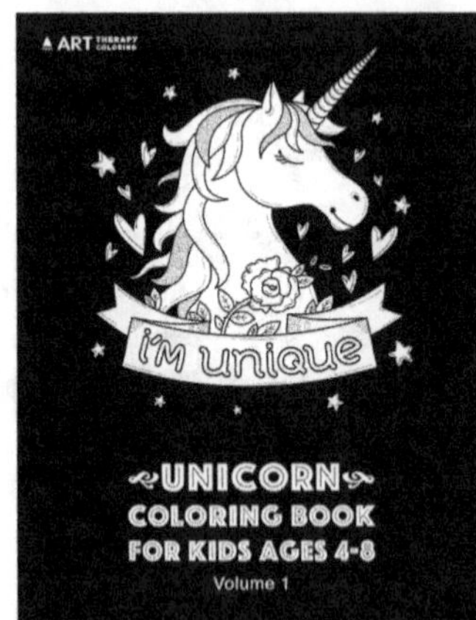

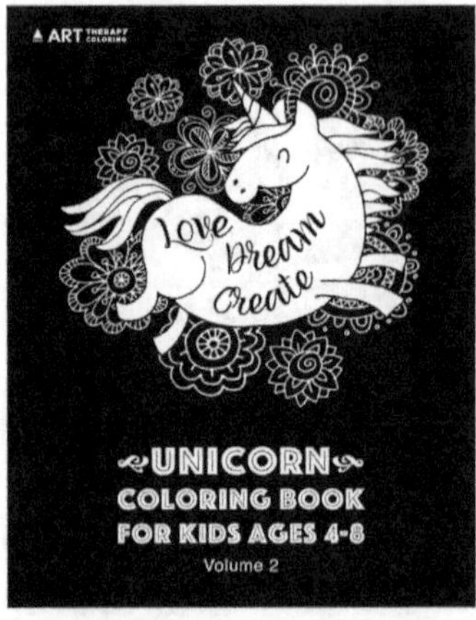

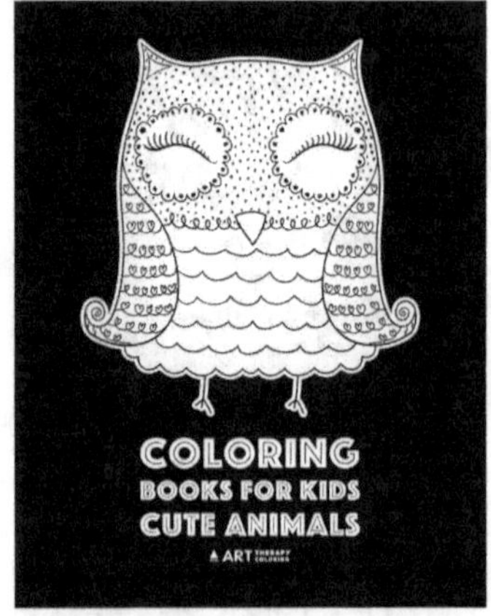

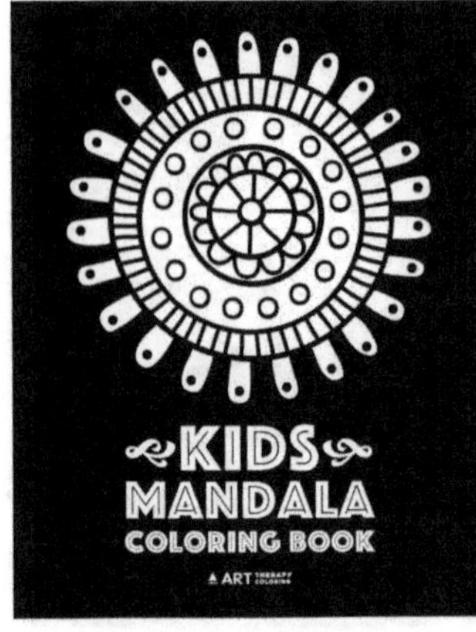

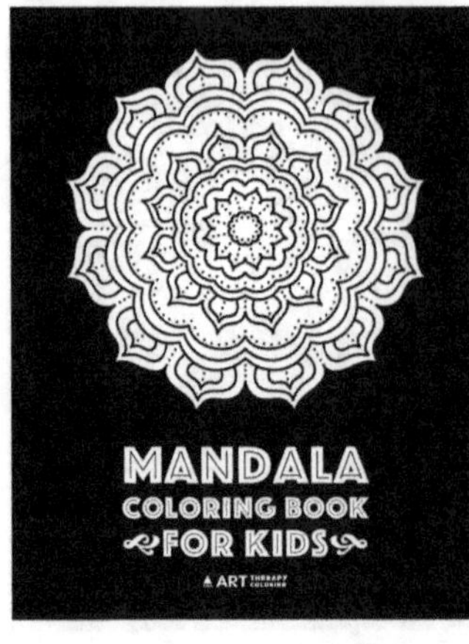

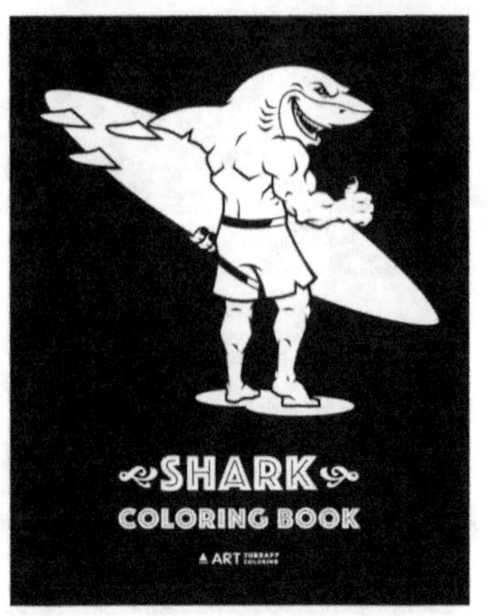

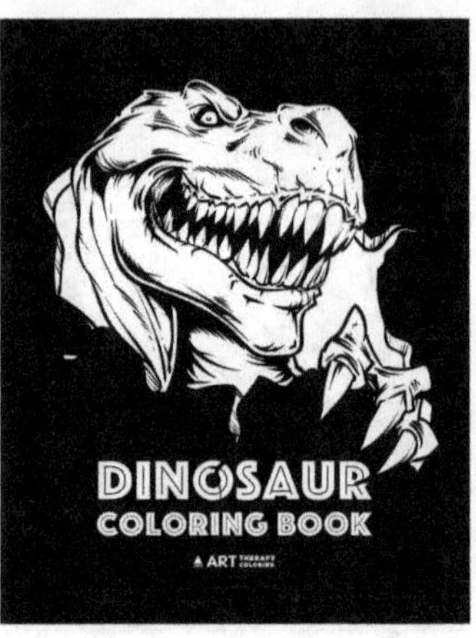

Coloring Books For Adults

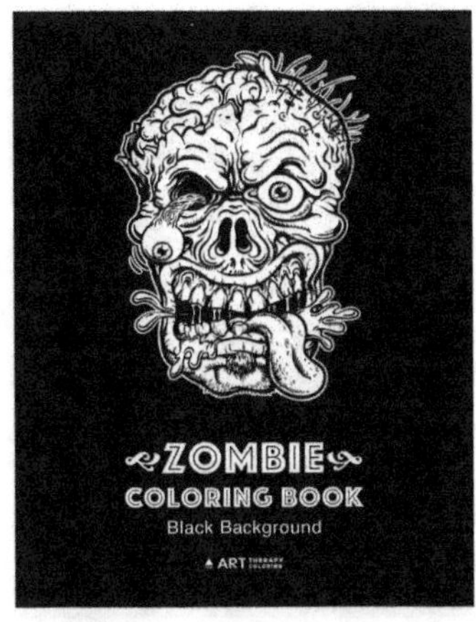

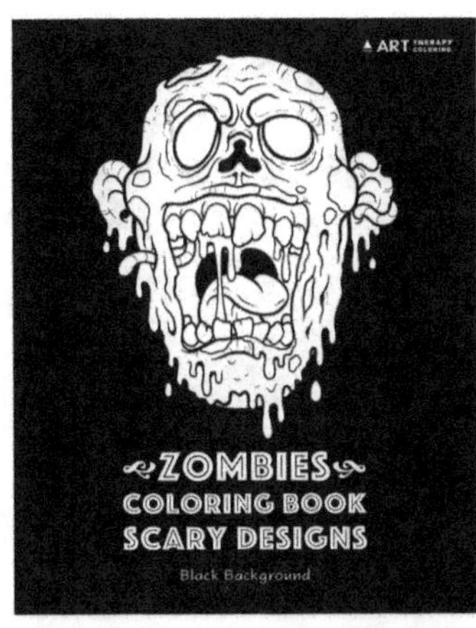

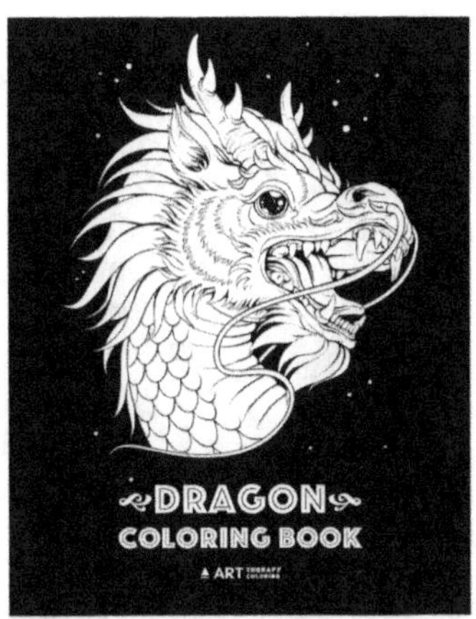

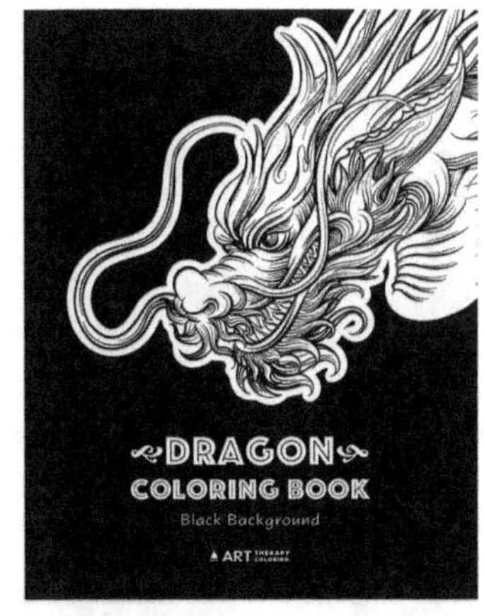

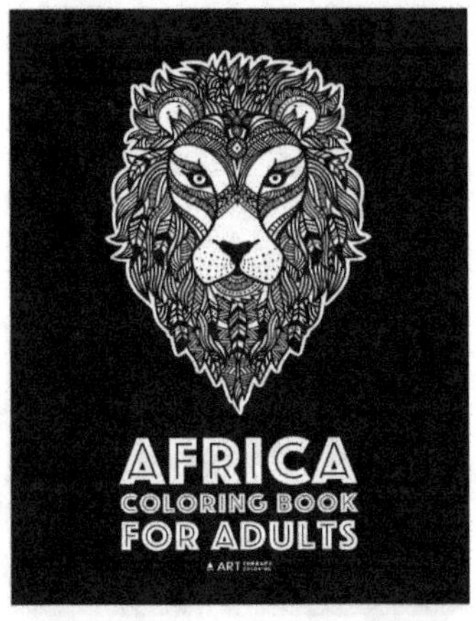

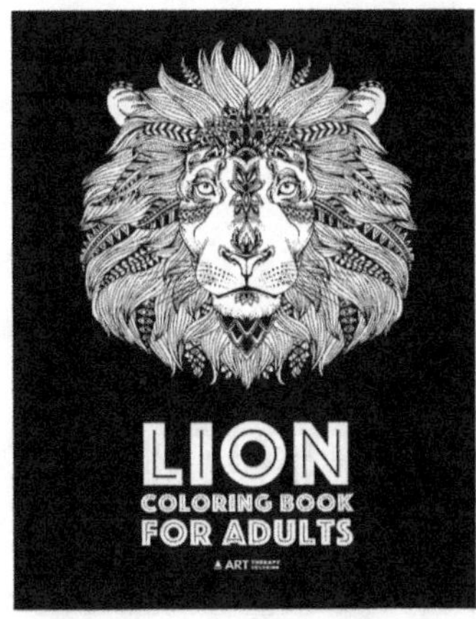

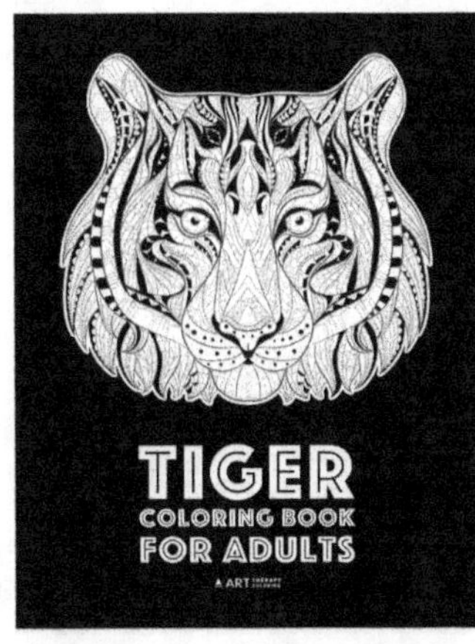

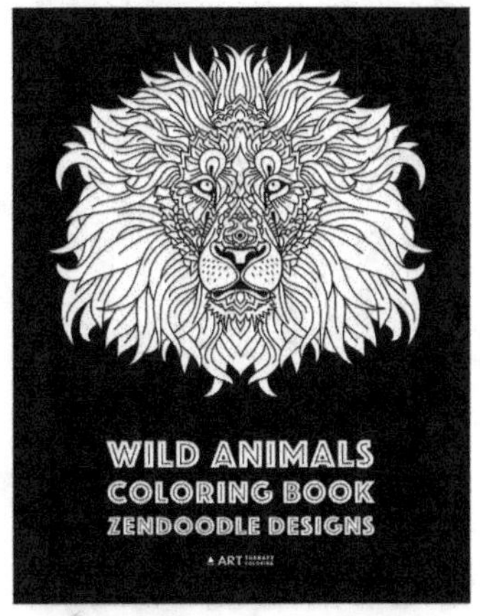

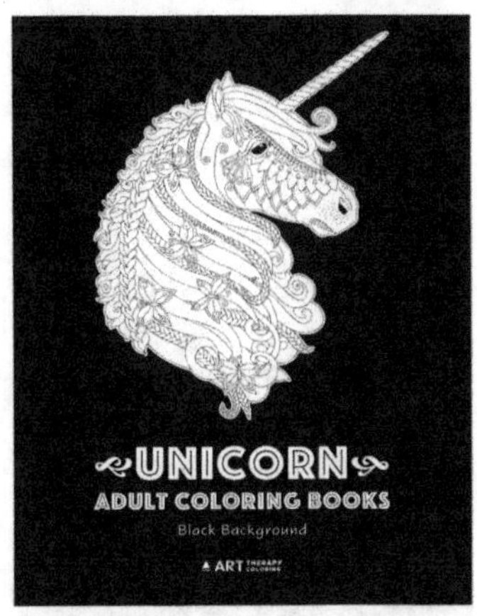

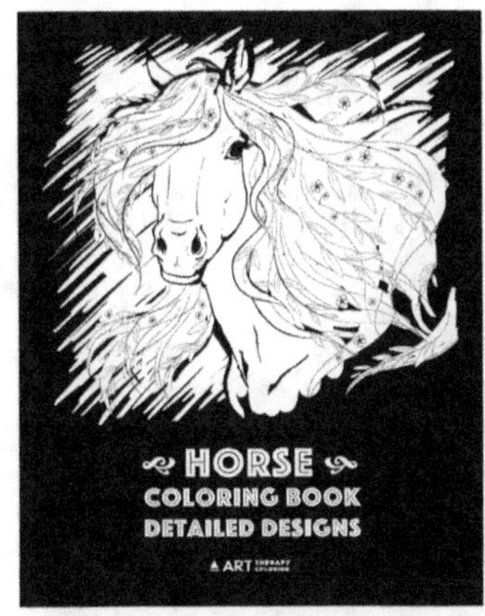

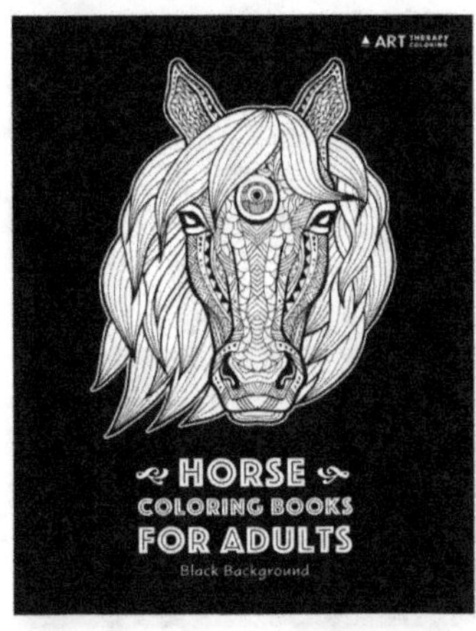

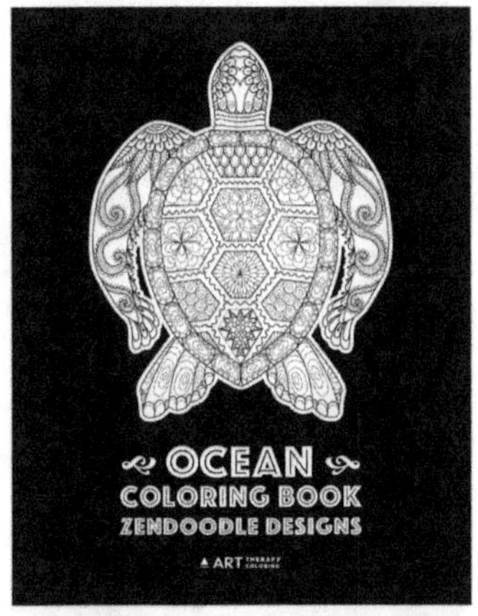

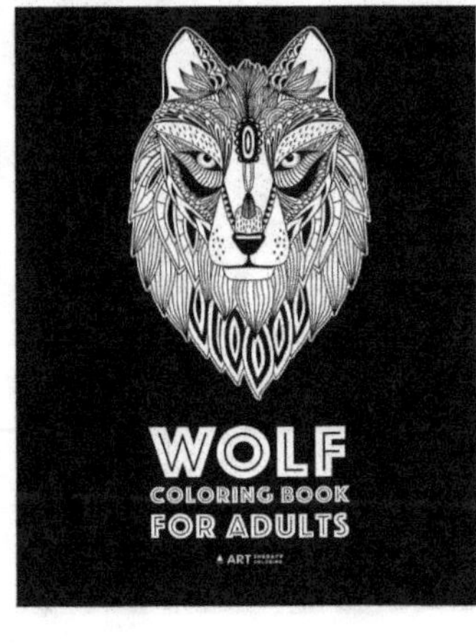

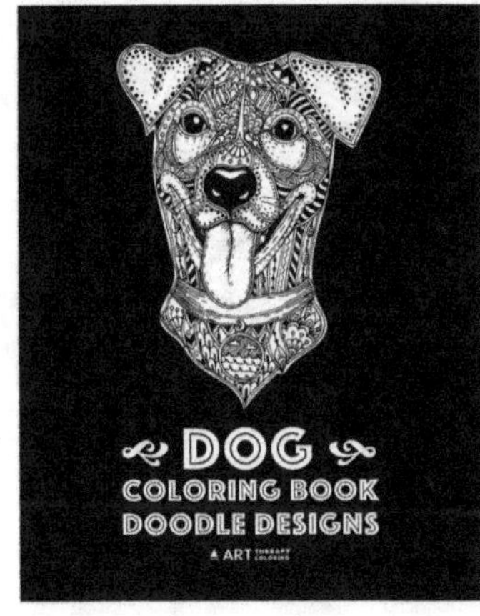

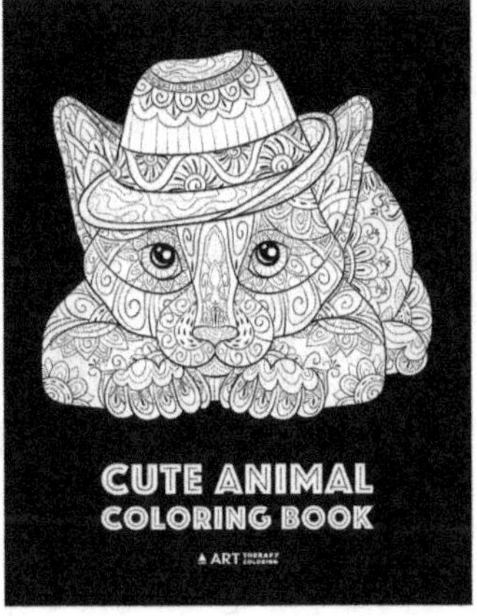

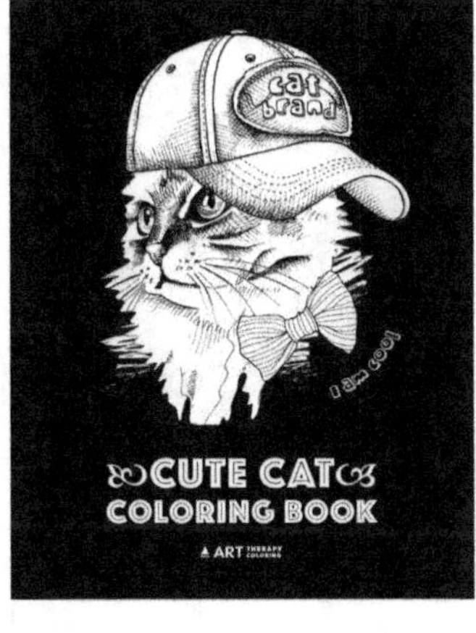

Coloring Books For Adults

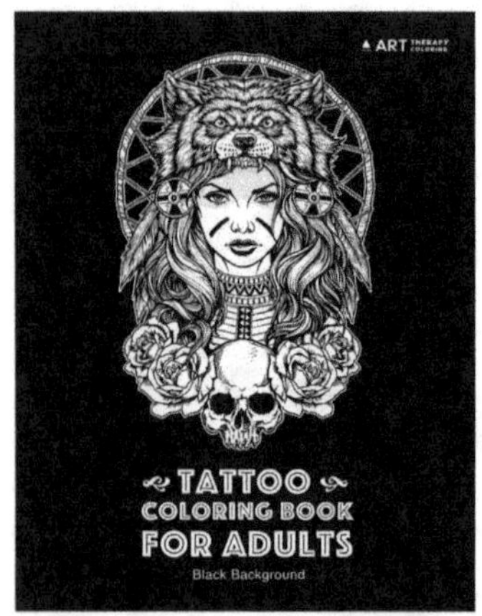

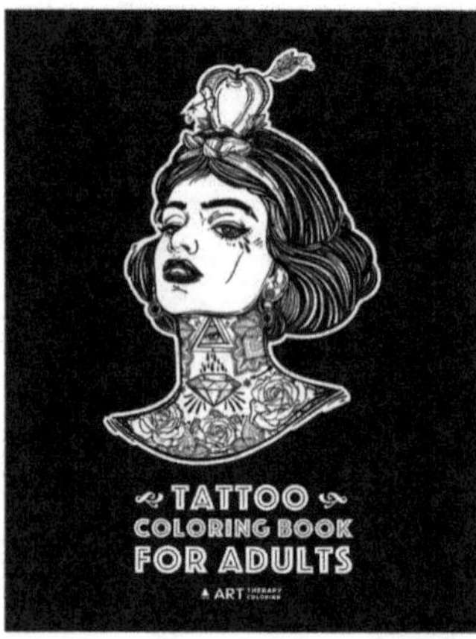

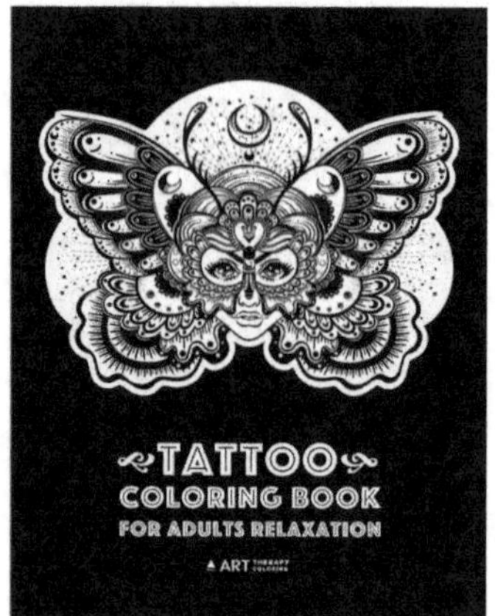

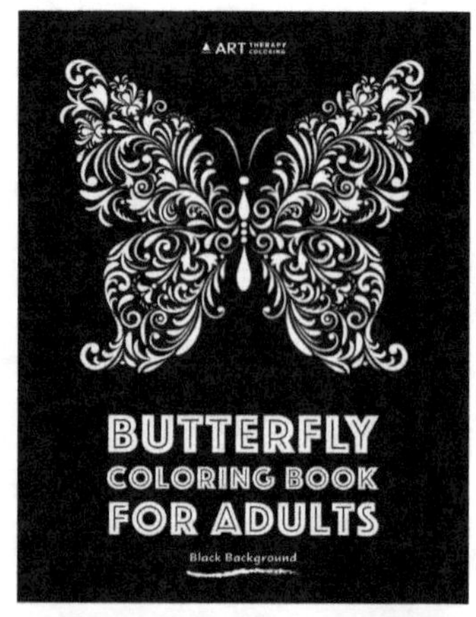

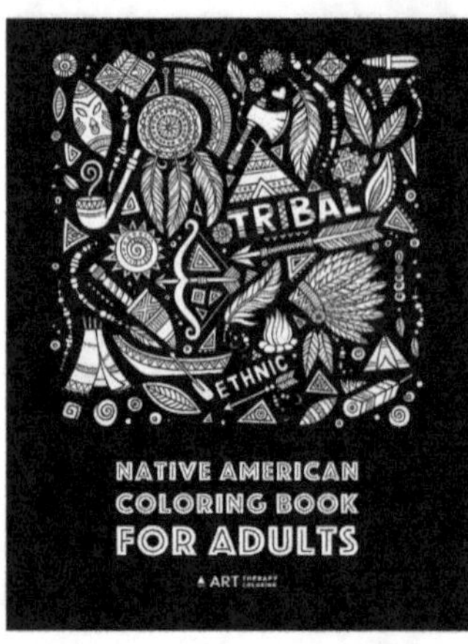

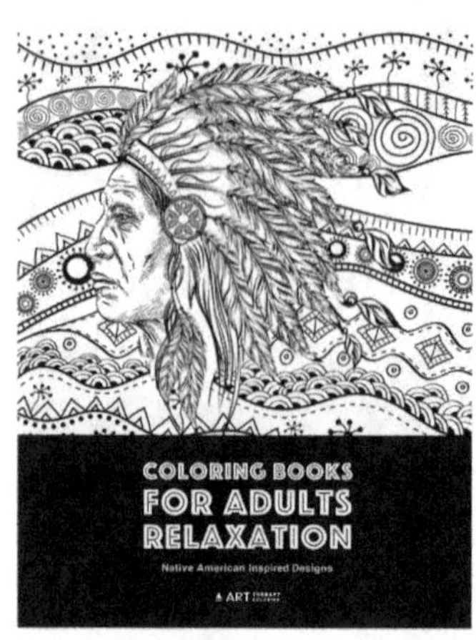

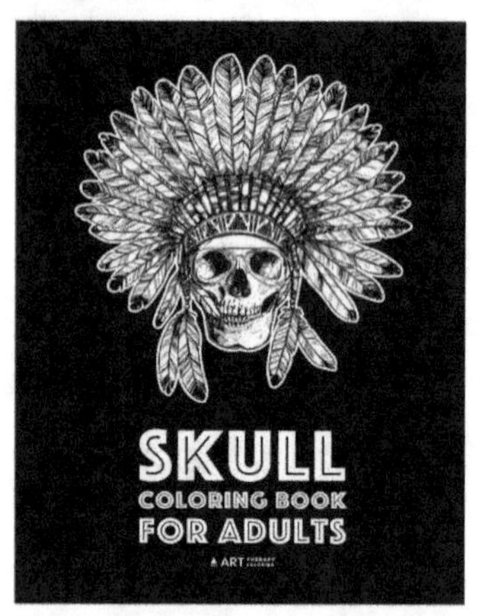

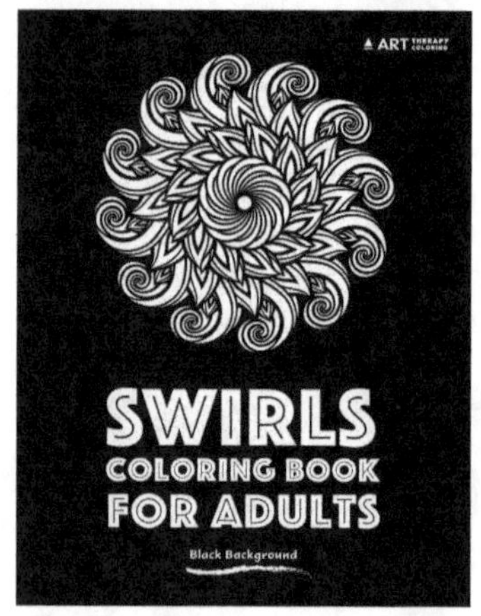

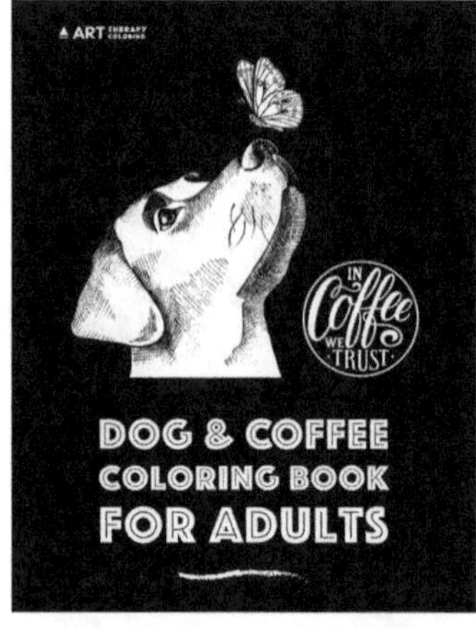

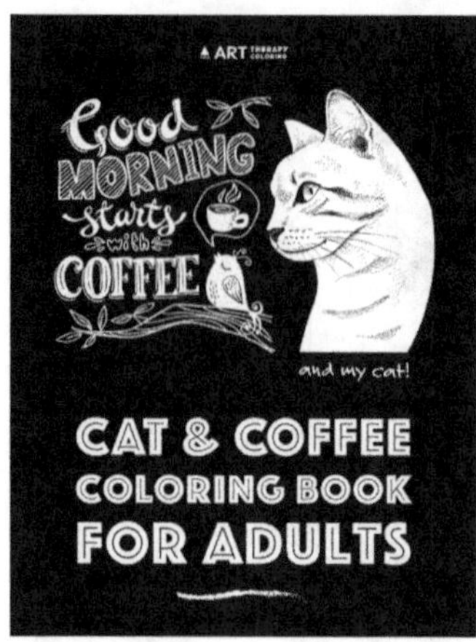

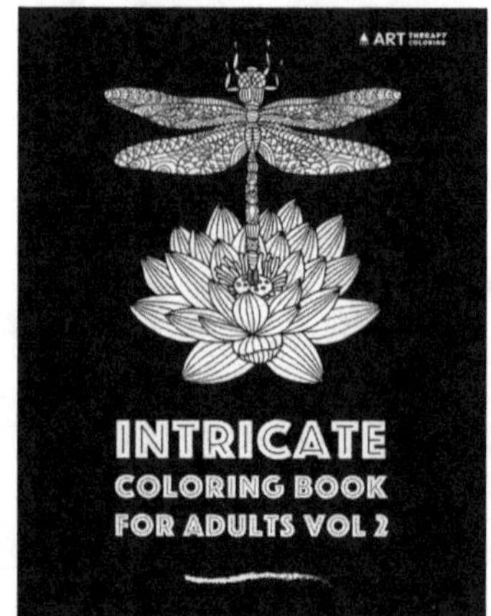

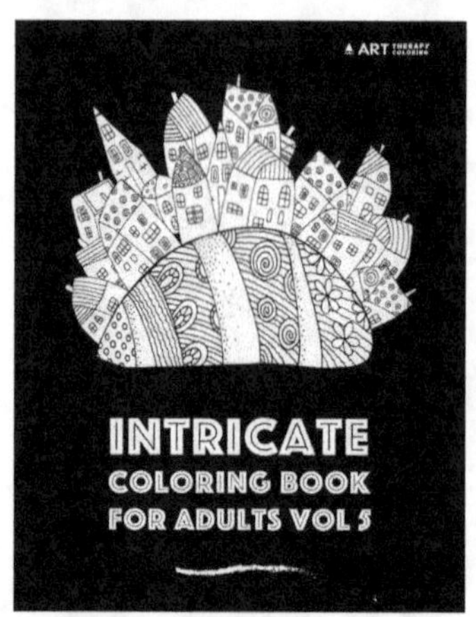

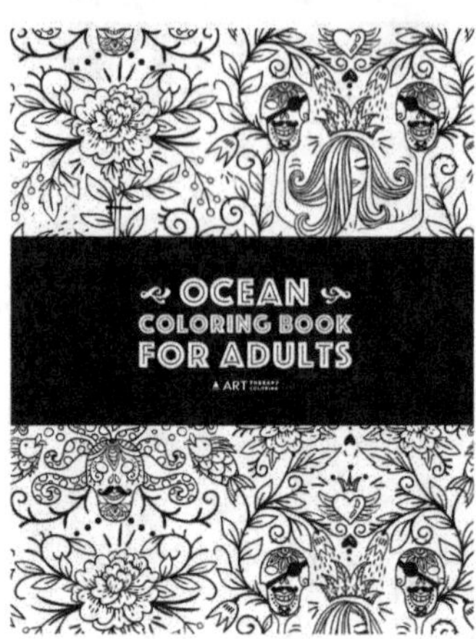

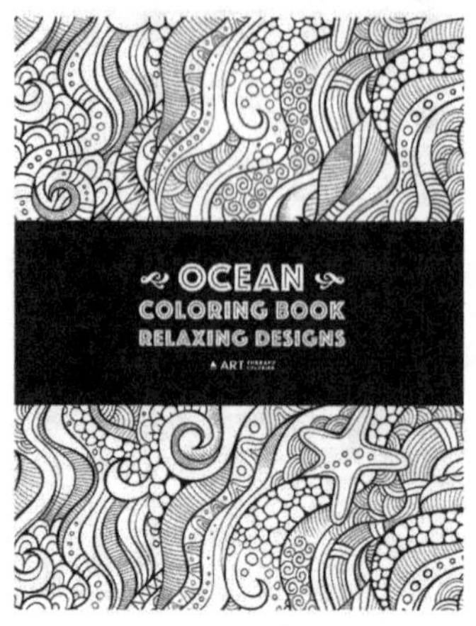

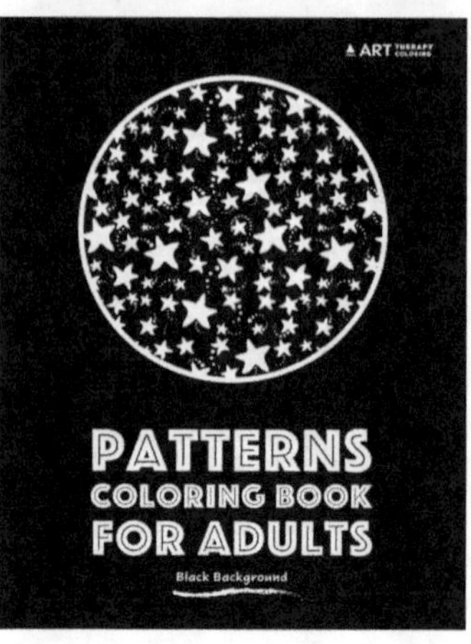

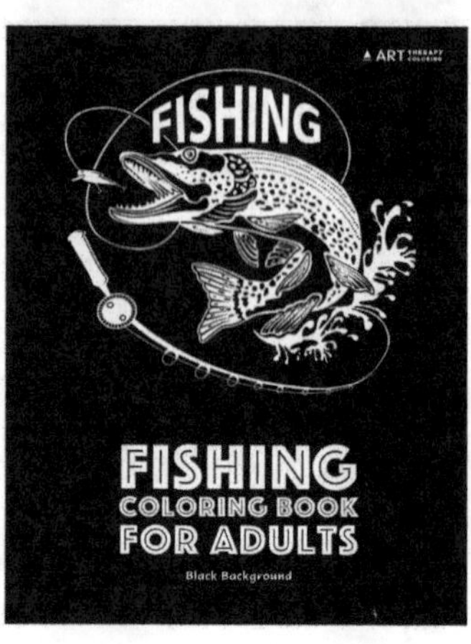

Coloring Books For Adults

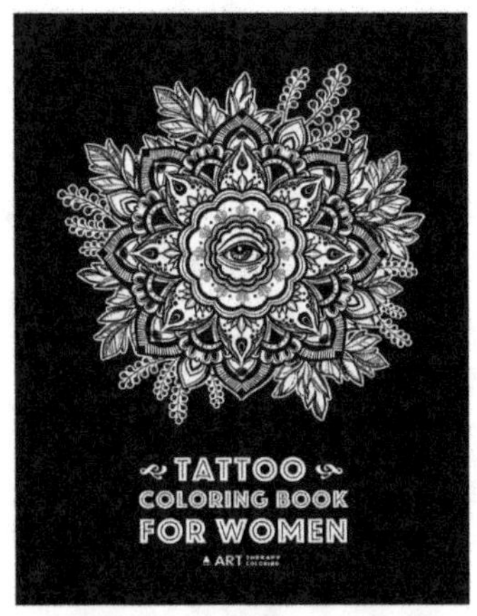

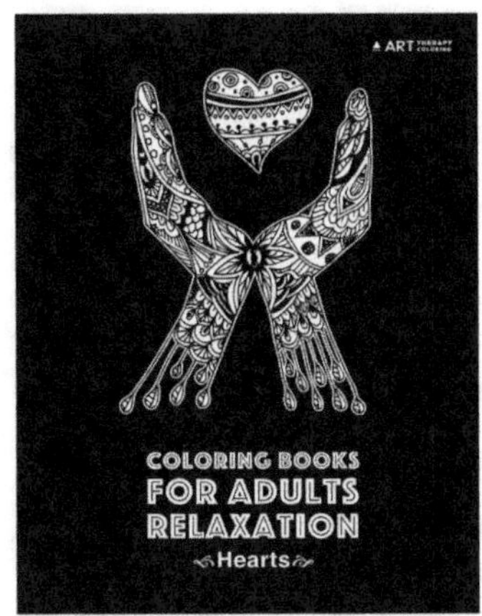

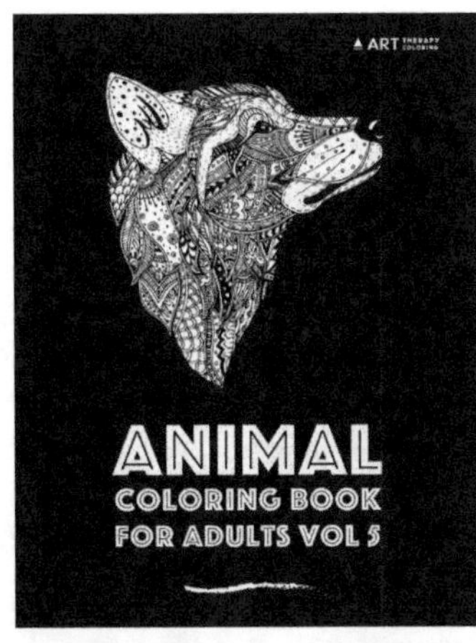

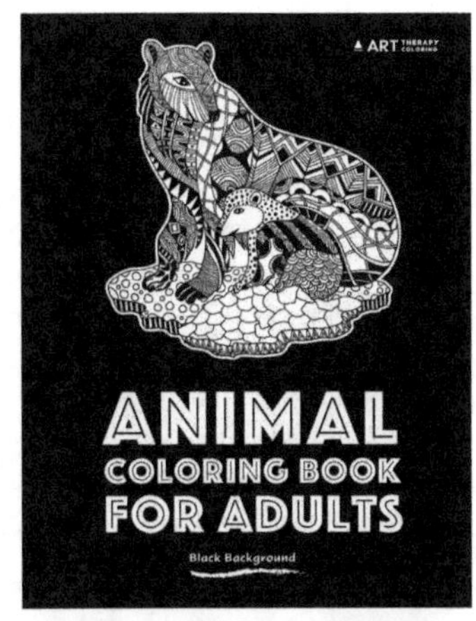

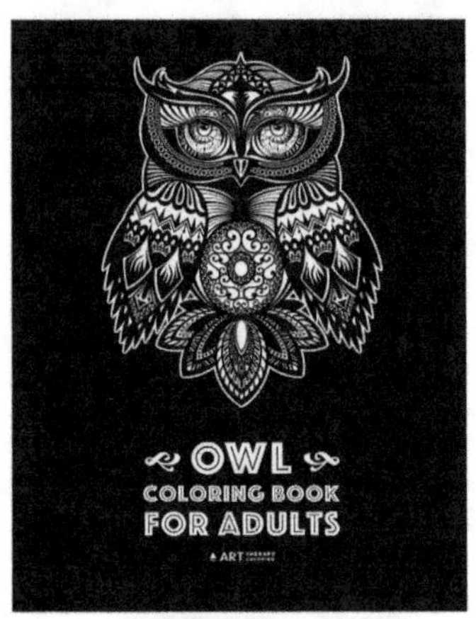

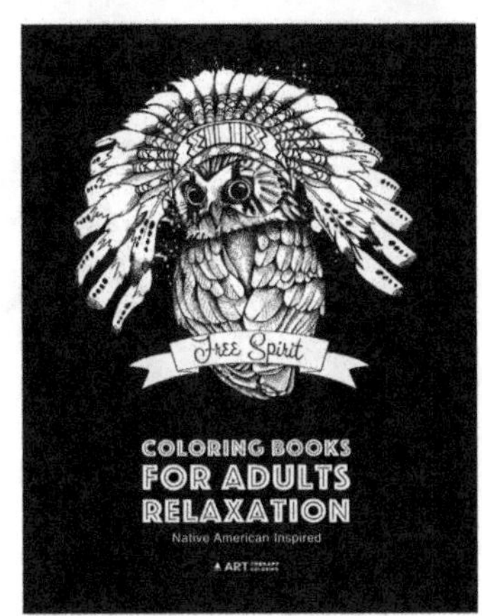

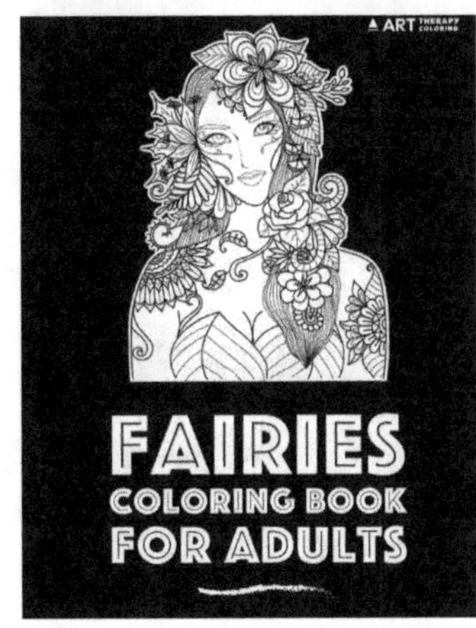

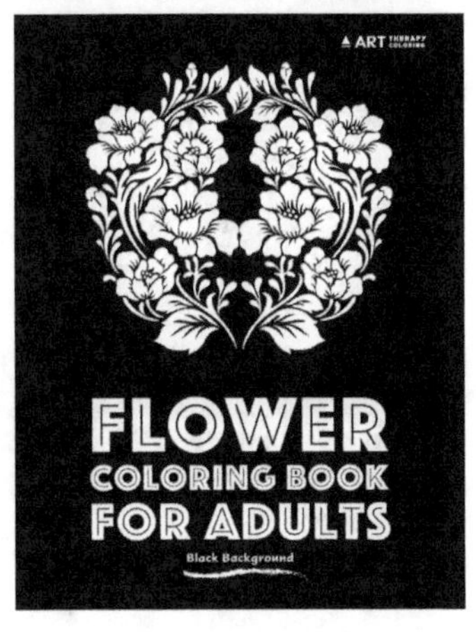

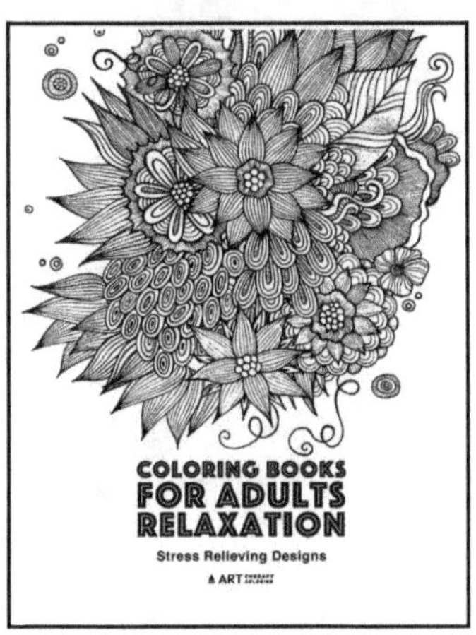

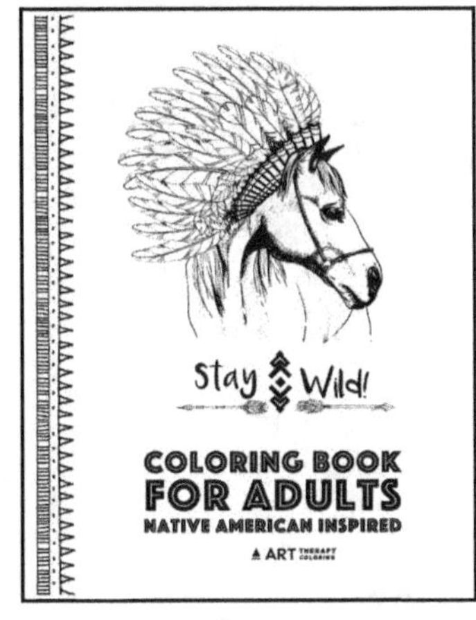

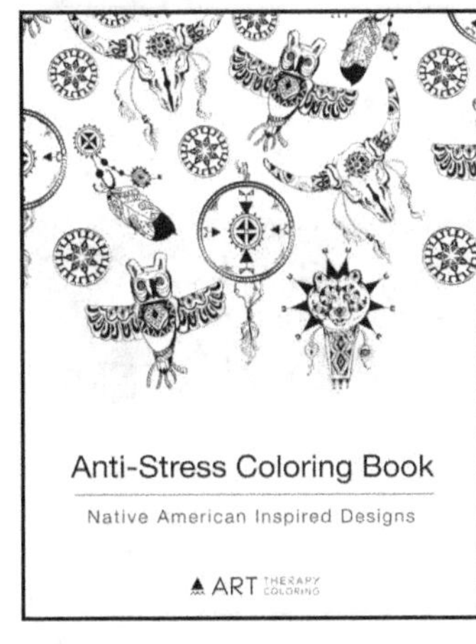

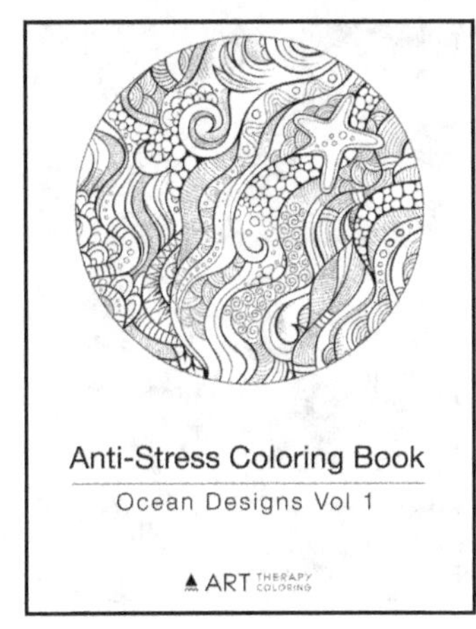

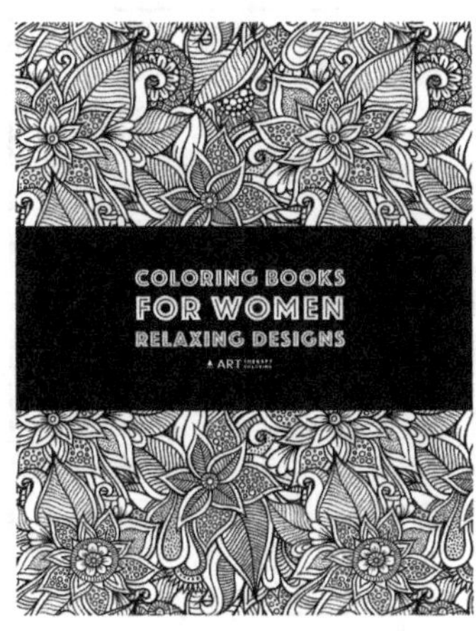

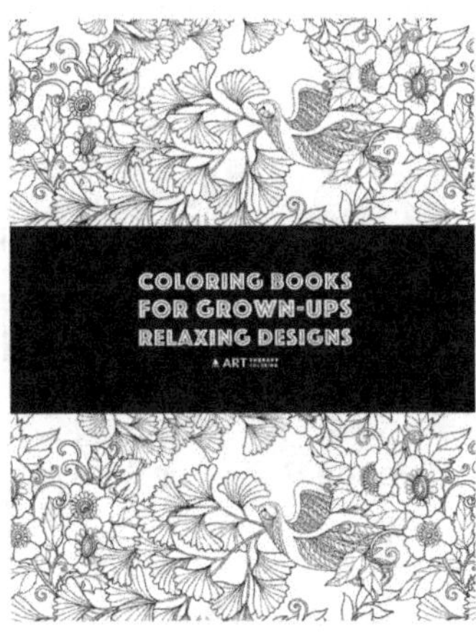

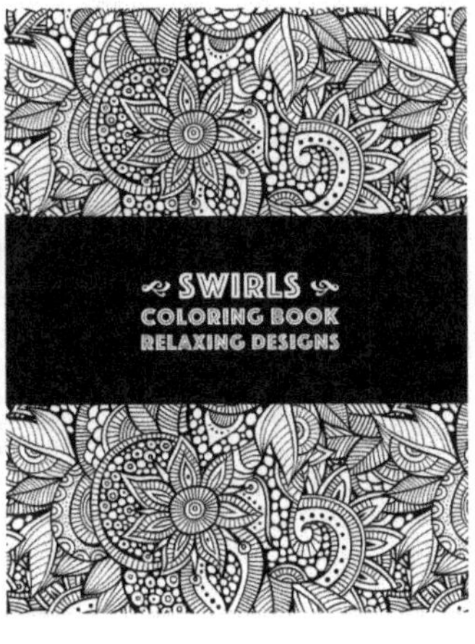

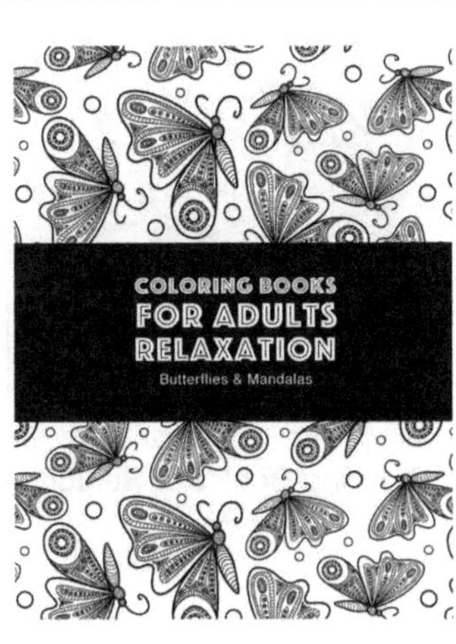

Coloring Books For Seniors

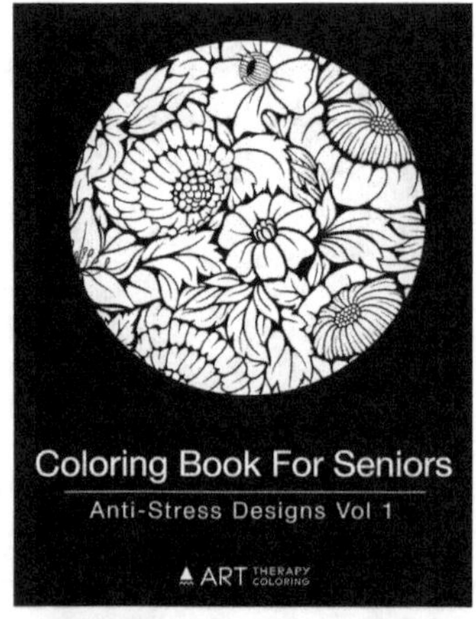

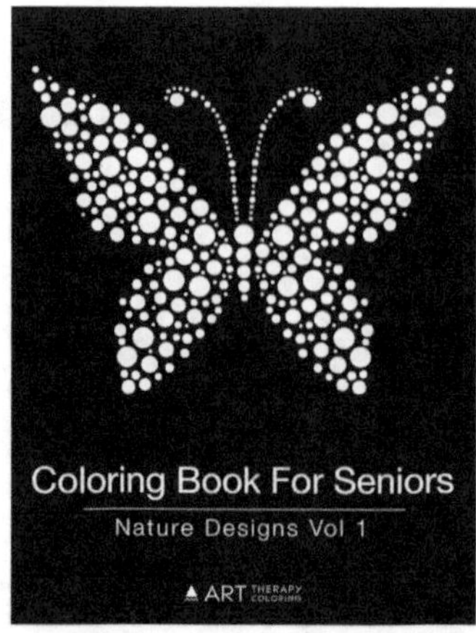

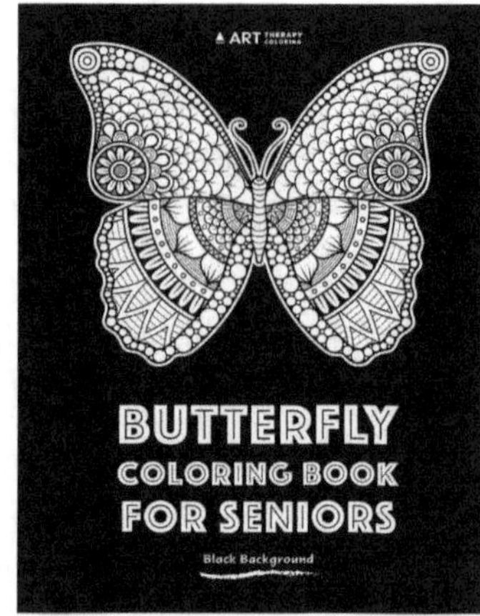

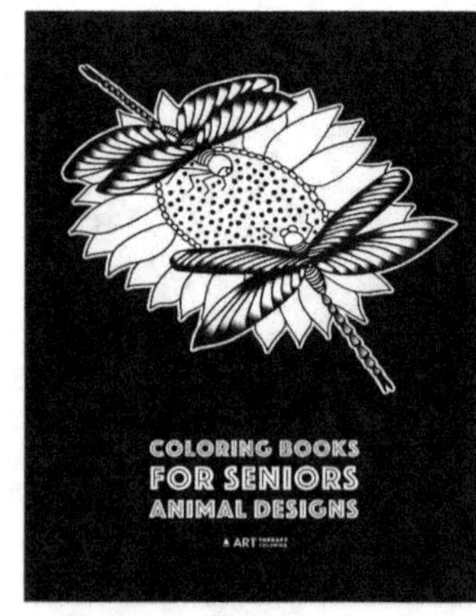

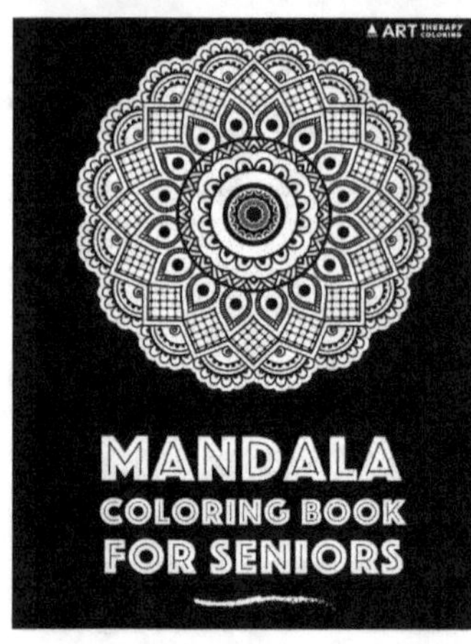

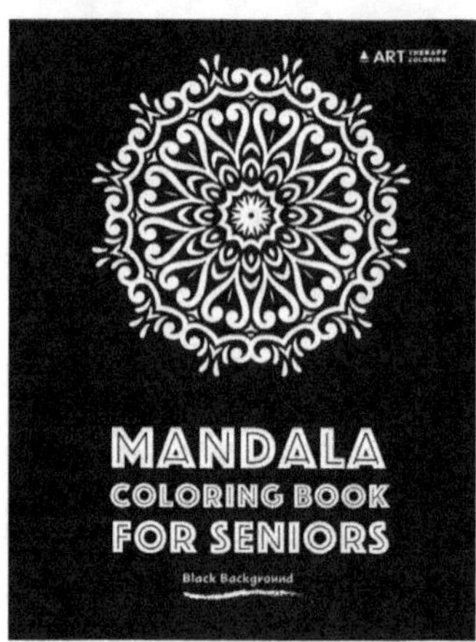

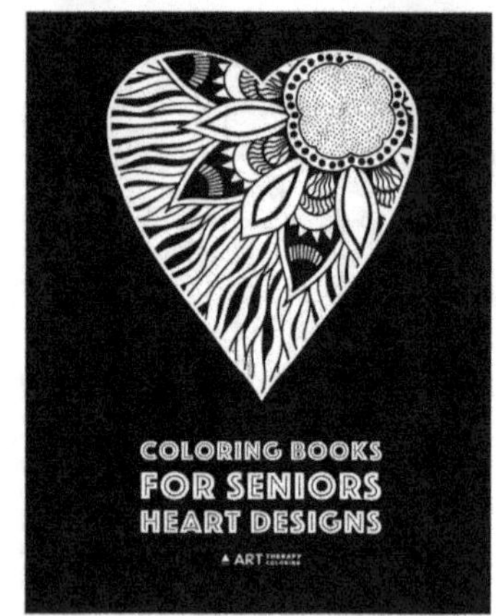

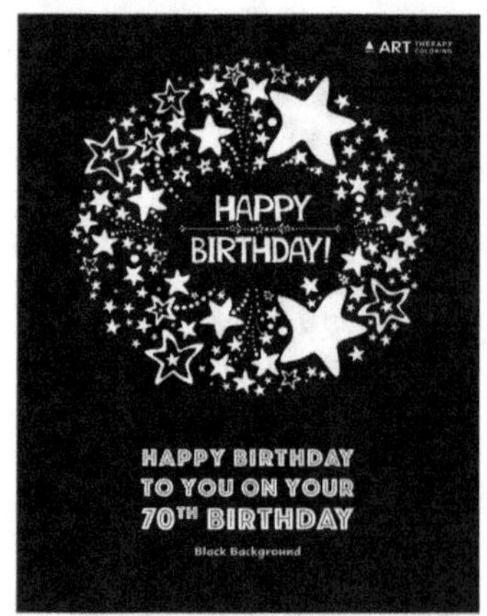

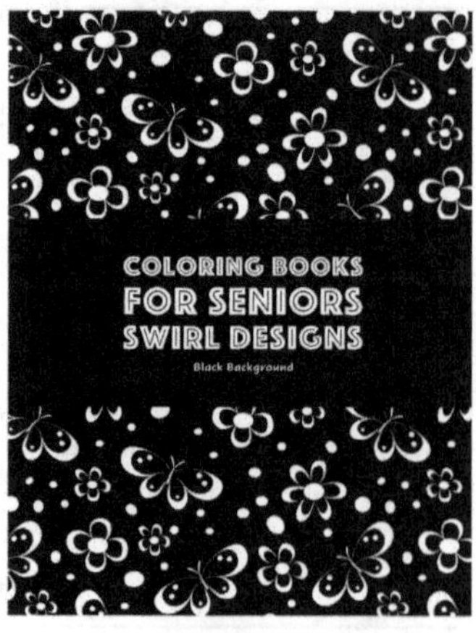

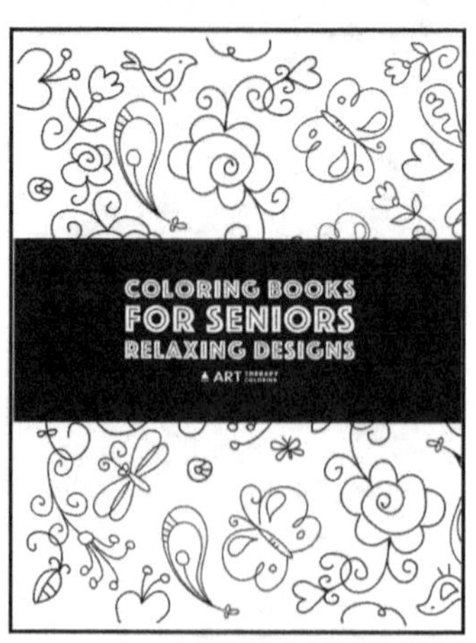

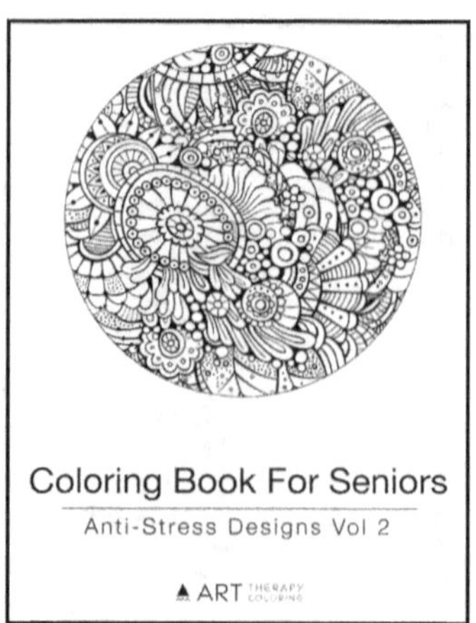

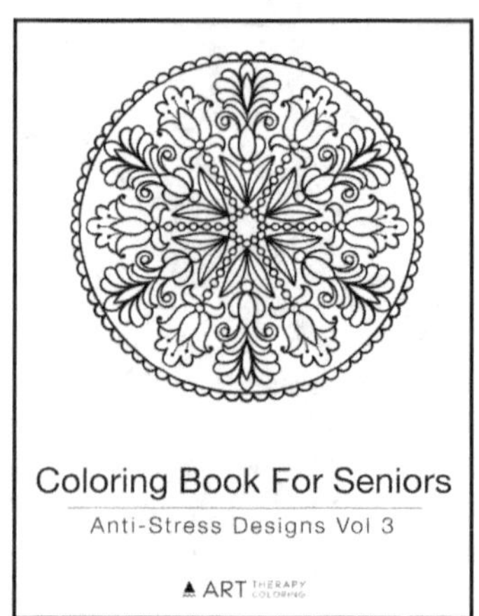

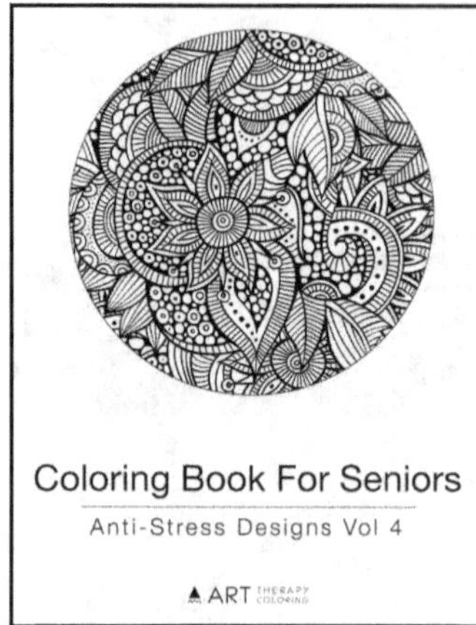

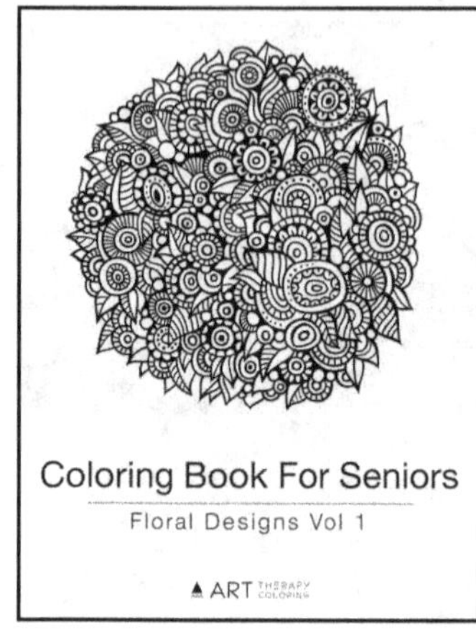

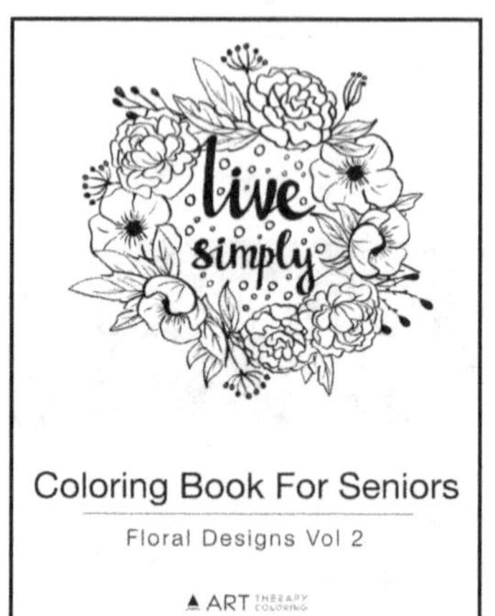

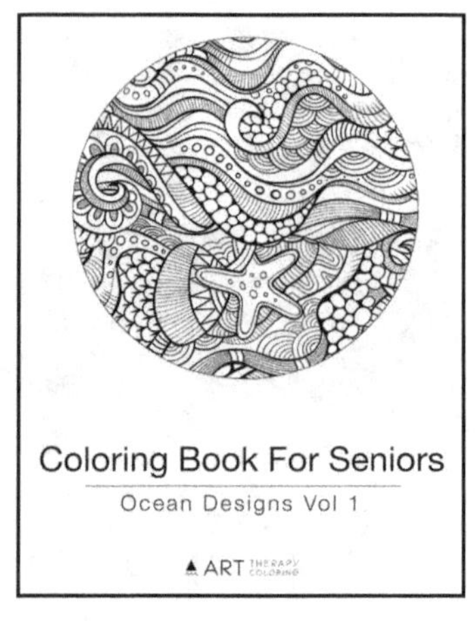

Coloring Books For Men

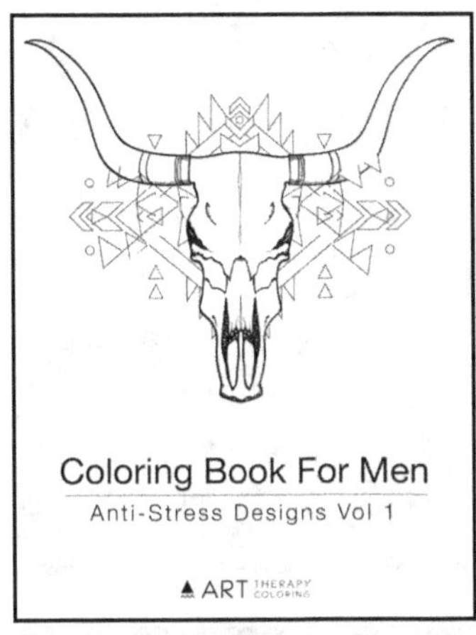

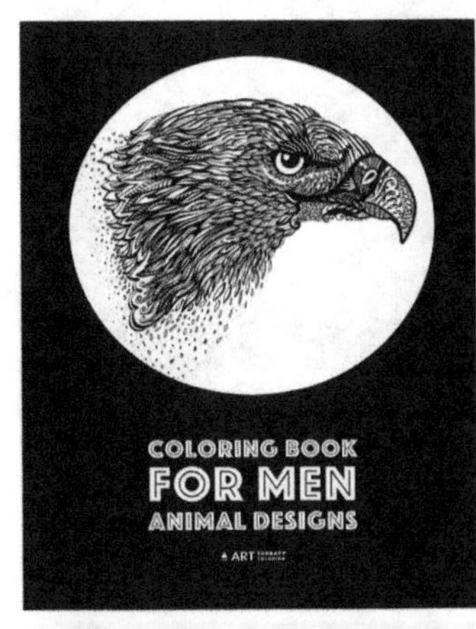

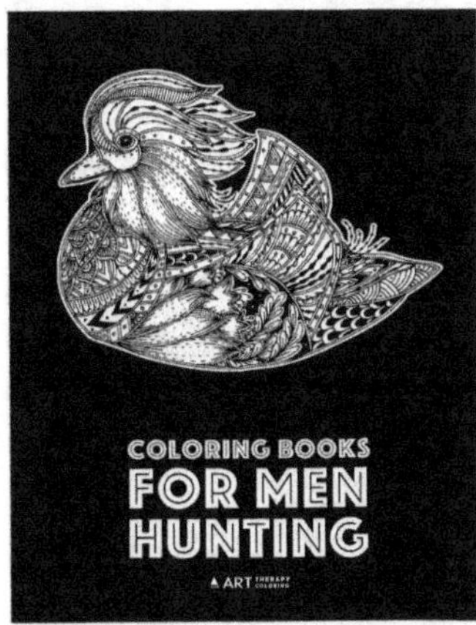

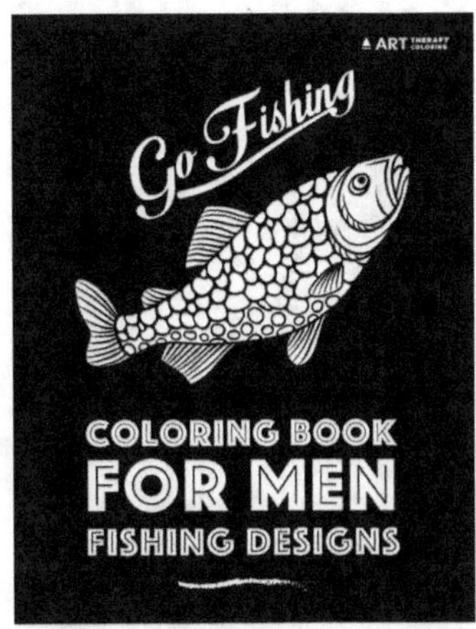

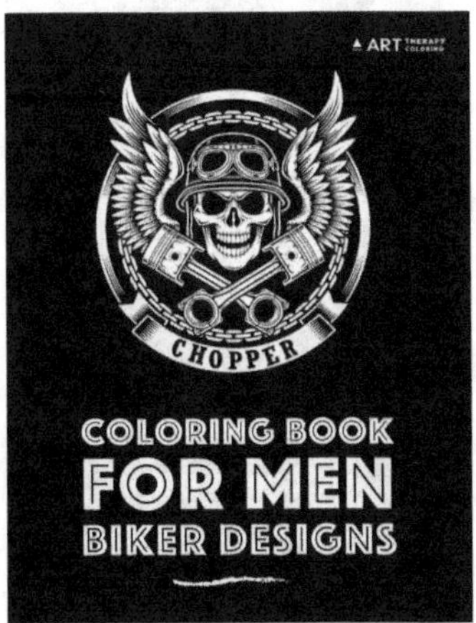

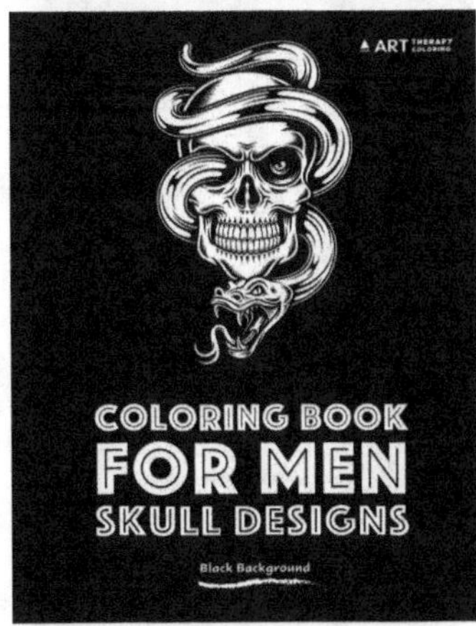

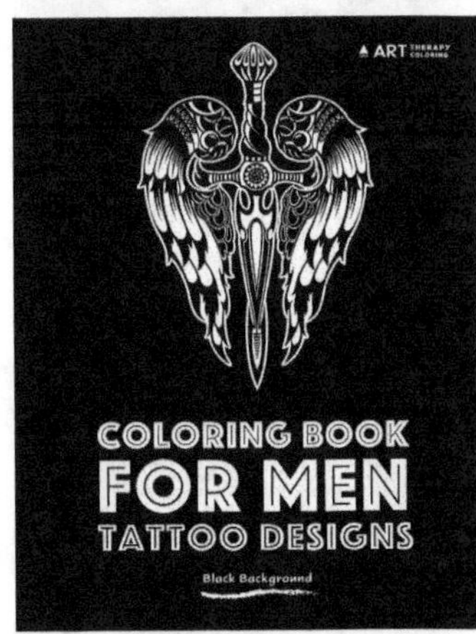

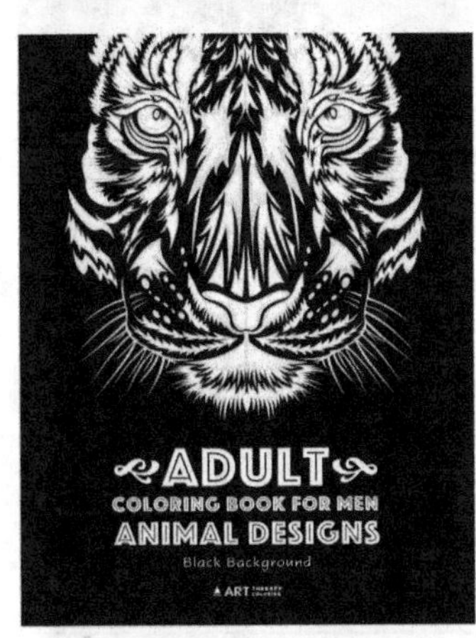

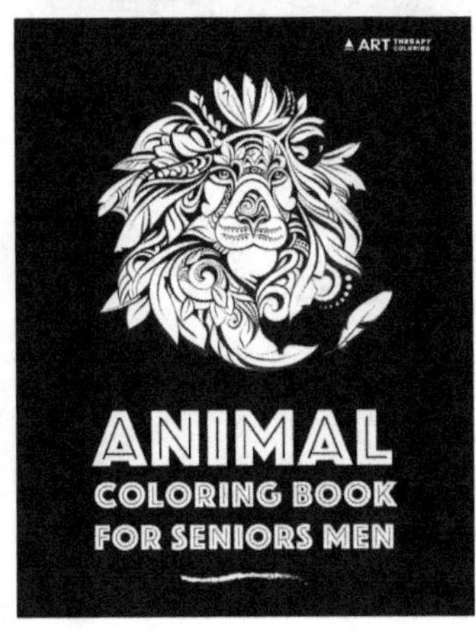

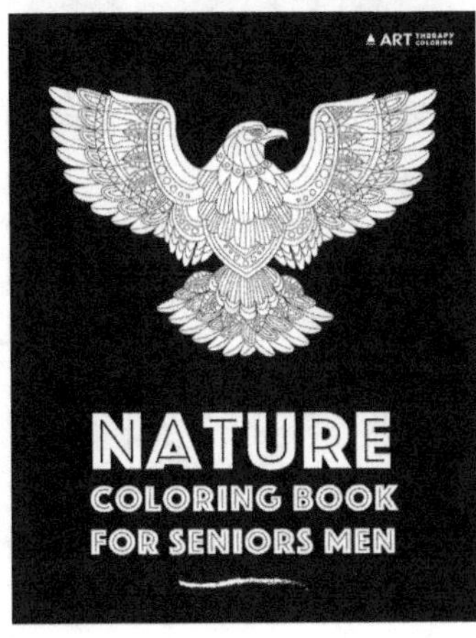

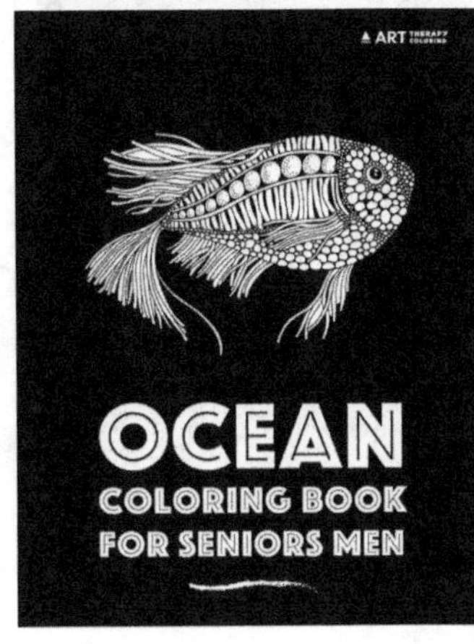

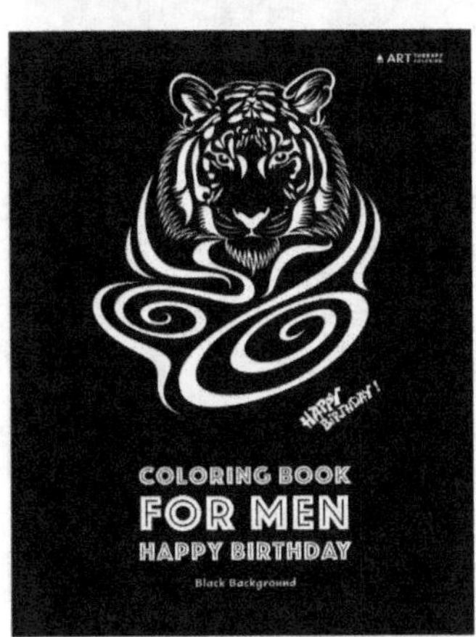

Coloring Books For Special Occasions

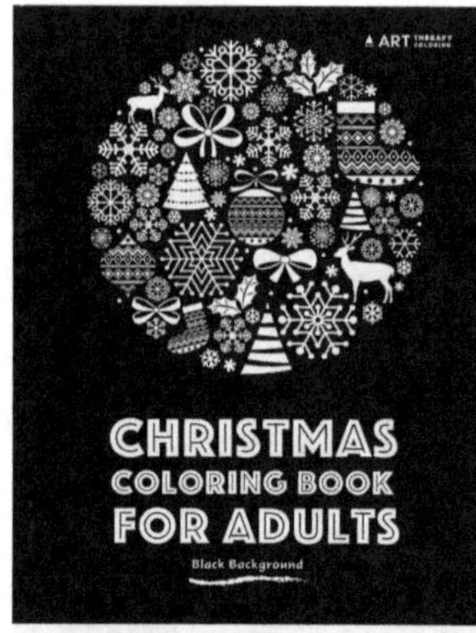
CHRISTMAS
COLORING BOOK
FOR ADULTS
Black Background

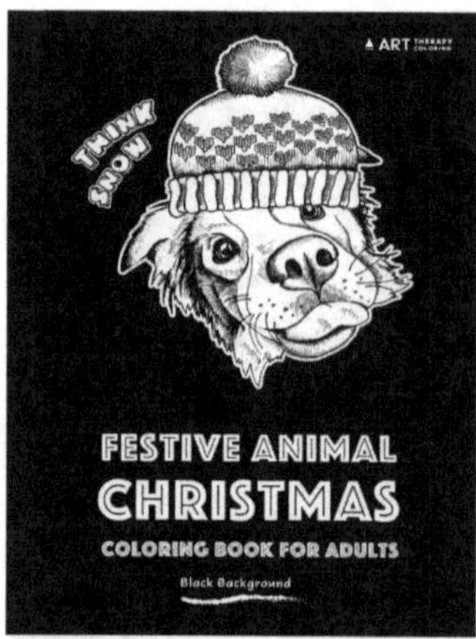
FESTIVE ANIMAL
CHRISTMAS
COLORING BOOK FOR ADULTS
Black Background

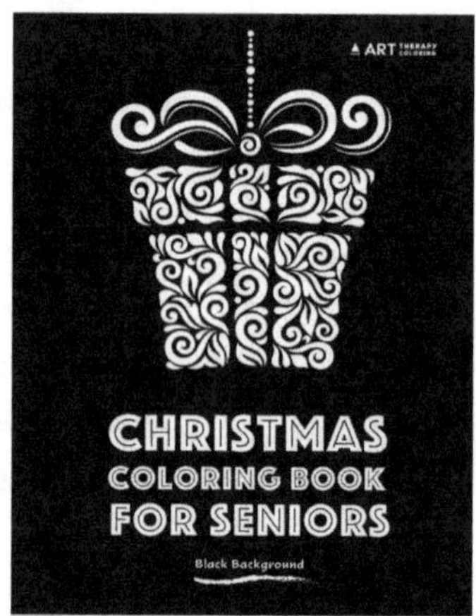
CHRISTMAS
COLORING BOOK
FOR SENIORS
Black Background

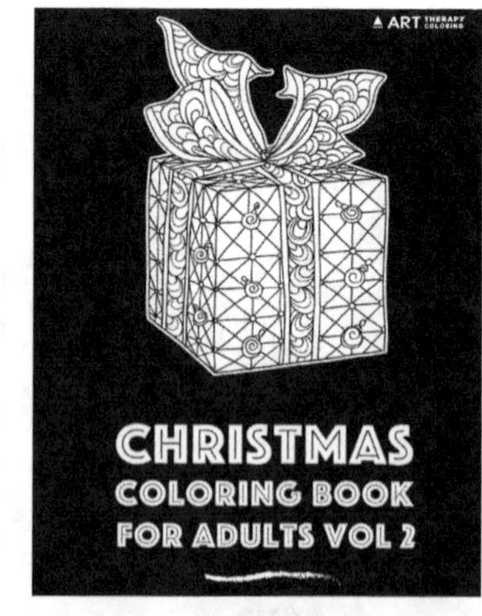
CHRISTMAS
COLORING BOOK
FOR ADULTS VOL 2

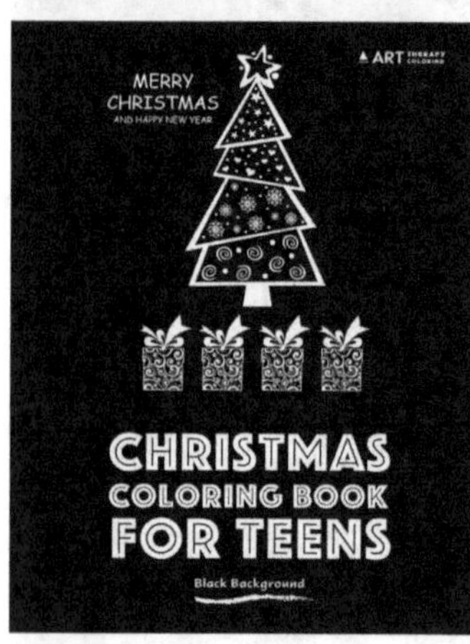
MERRY
CHRISTMAS
CHRISTMAS
COLORING BOOK
FOR TEENS
Black Background

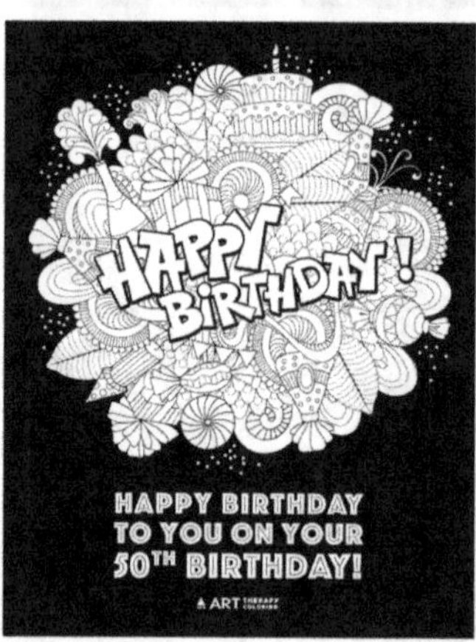
HAPPY BIRTHDAY!
HAPPY BIRTHDAY
TO YOU ON YOUR
50TH BIRTHDAY!

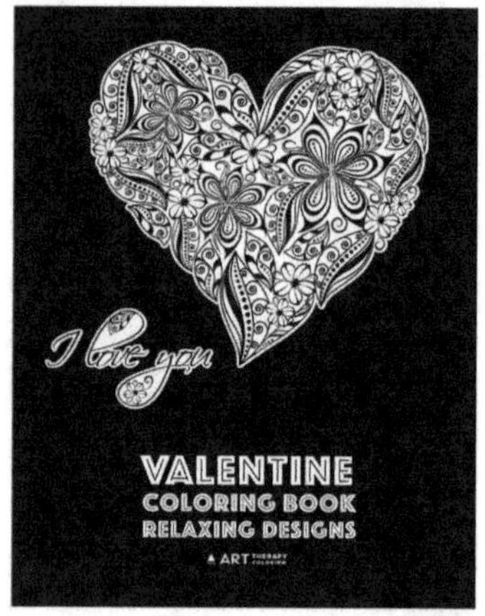
I love you
VALENTINE
COLORING BOOK
RELAXING DESIGNS

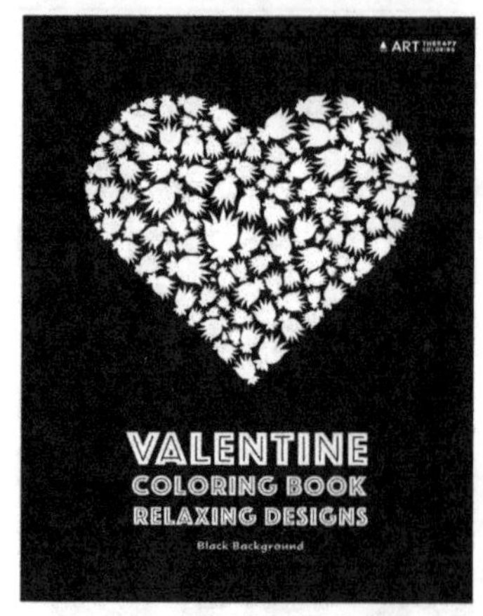
VALENTINE
COLORING BOOK
RELAXING DESIGNS
Black Background

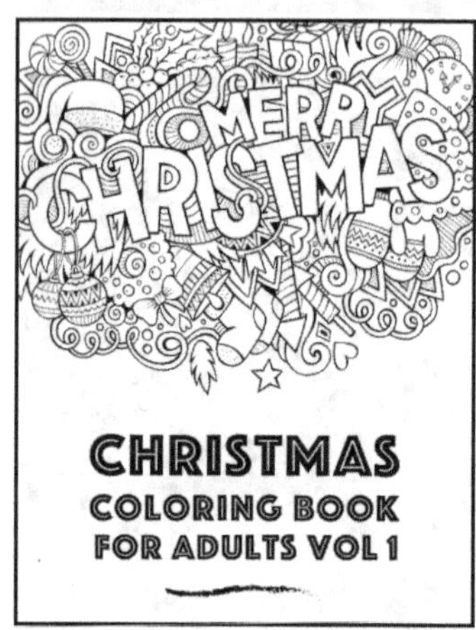
MERRY
CHRISTMAS
CHRISTMAS
COLORING BOOK
FOR ADULTS VOL 1

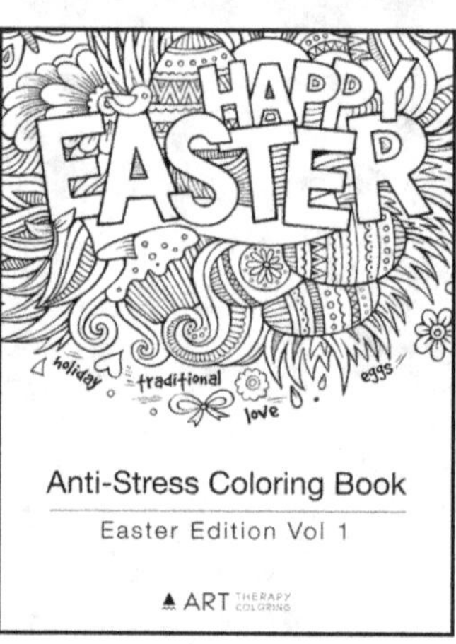
HAPPY
EASTER
holiday
traditional
love
eggs
Anti-Stress Coloring Book
Easter Edition Vol 1
ART

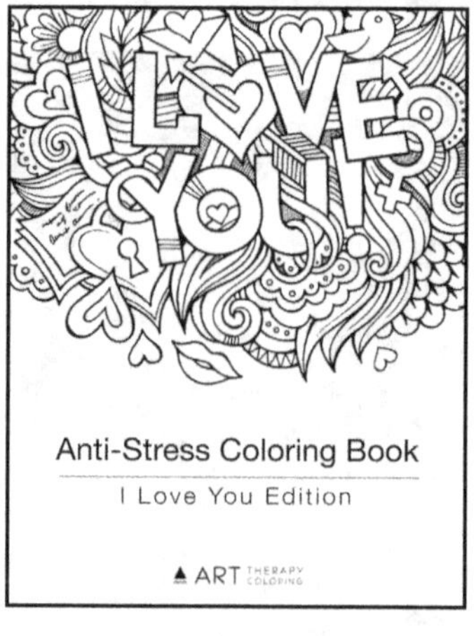
I LOVE YOU!
Anti-Stress Coloring Book
I Love You Edition
ART

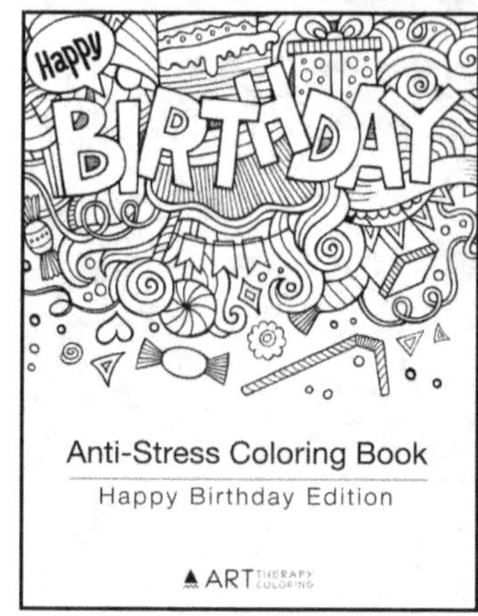
Happy
BIRTHDAY
Anti-Stress Coloring Book
Happy Birthday Edition
ART

Coloring Book For Teens
Anti-Stress Designs Vol 1

Published by:
Art Therapy Coloring
El Dorado Hills, California
www.arttherapycoloring.com

Shutterstock Images

ISBN: 978-1-944427-16-0

www.ingramcontent.com/pod-product-compliance
Lightning Source LLC
LaVergne TN
LVHW080335110826
845155LV00027B/246

9781944427160